RAISED FOR RICHNE$$

Teaching kids
money skills
for life

KARYN HODGENS

ISBN: 0-615-34016-4
ISBN-13: 9780615340166
Library of Congress Control Number: 2010920105

About the Author

Karyn Hodgens studied child development at Chico State University before receiving her master's degree in education with a specialization in elementary mathematics. With a multiple-subjects teaching credential, for over two decades, her passion has been to create engaging curriculum and in 2006, Hodgens co-founded Kidnexions, a kids' educational company. In partnership with her husband, John, she created KidsSave, a kids' savings and money management software program designed as a tool to help parents teach their children how to save and spend money wisely. Currently, she continues to teach kids how to prepare for their financial futures in addition to writing about kids and money issues. *Raised for Richness* is her first book. You can visit Karyn online at www.kidnexions.com or email her at karyn@kidnexions.com.

About the Illustrator

Bryn Hobson is a student and future graphic designer bent on changing the world. He wants to create design that still feels human in a generation of digital clutter. Simply, he hopes to use his skills to start discussion about the issues in the world. In the meantime, he enjoys music, art, and beautiful friendships in the lovely state of California. Visit him online at www.brynhobson.com.

Praise for *Raised for Richness*

"I highly recommend that every parent sit down with their children and go through *Raised for Richness* together. It is filled with practical activities that will help your family create a game plan on important issues such as: how to handle allowance, developing a workable savings plan, getting your child thinking about investing and much more. When you complete this workbook, you can feel good knowing that the lessons you have picked up and shared with your son or daughter will benefit them for a lifetime."
>> Vince Shorb, National Youth Financial Educators Council

"When it comes to talking to kids about money, most parents fumble the ball. There are everyday opportunities to teach our children the financial ABCs, and this book provides plenty of useful pointers on how to broach the topic. Not only will your children benefit in the long run by developing money smarts at a young age, but Mom and Dad might learn a thing or two as well about saving, budgeting, and setting goals."
>> Steve Rosen, nationally syndicated author of the "Kids & Money" column and an assistant business editor at *The Kansas City Star*

"I found myself nodding in agreement with Karyn Hodgens' book *Raised for Richness*. Her philosophy is in tune with my own on such things as giving an allowance, teaching kids to save, and using debit and credit cards. And Hodgens hits the nail on the head when she says that kids like it when it's all about them. Or as I like to put it, parents need to learn to think like a kid. Hodgens gives them plenty of opportunities with hands-on, family-friendly activities and conversation starters."
>> Janet Bodnar, Kiplinger's Personal Finance Editor

"My husband and I found the book to be extremely busy parent friendly. It was balanced, clear, and we were able to implement the strategies immediately."
>> Yvonne Edwards, parent and third grade teacher

"After reading the section on earning money, my son got a job picking up pinecones for the neighbor. She offered five cents per pinecone with placement in a green can on her driveway. 30 pinecones = $1.50. He loved it!"
>> Marcie Colletti, parent

"What a GREAT guide, very common sense, down to earth, and VALUE BASED. It is to be used over and over again for years, with dialogue ideas that should occur regularly. The activities and worksheets really help US focus on what's important, as well as our son, and they really helped guide us in helping him create a way to be responsible and effective in creating money goals, NEEDS vs WANTS, and good guidelines to establish effective behaviors for himself."
Juliana and Randy Orrick, parents

"I really like how the approach is not just on money but on values."
Ingrid Parry, parent

"Giving the girls an allowance and making them responsible for their own money and personal expenses was immediately effective after the first store trip. The kids already questioned if a trinket was worth spending their money on. We've been searching for an effective way to handle allowances. This has been great!"
Lisa Johnson, parent and third grade teacher

"We love how the book is organized and it prompted my husband and me to have good conversations about our money philosophy."
Erin Givans, parent

"Thinking about my childhood money experiences certainly solidified/clarified impressions that I had of my young exposure to money. The best thing it did was to emphasize that we need to give the boys some money to manage."
Jim and Kim Fagundes, parents

"I like the many examples and worksheets provided in the book. They make it easier to implement the suggestions and ideas."
Lynn and James Fox, parents

"*Raised for Richness* not only offers practical, easy money-handling advice for both parents and children: Ms. Hodgens' book reads as if one is speaking to a good friend while waiting in the carpool line at school, or chatting casually over coffee. The voice is familiar and unpretentious, and the lessons brief and easy to comprehend. *Raised for Richness* will give confidence to any parent ready to teach their children about the principles and values of money through actions, rather than simply words."
Patty Golditch, parent and librarian

Acknowledgements

The Families: I am forever thankful to all the field-test families who brought the manuscript pages of this book into their homes and put them through the ultimate test. Although I have been doing the activities for many years with my students in a classroom environment, it was "real" families integrating the activities into their everyday lives that was important for this book to be successful.

I was overwhelmed by the effort and consideration each family took to document their thoughts and experiences throughout the project. By the time I had finished reading all the questionnaires, I felt like I knew each one of their kids. The comments and suggestions, and even all the little anecdotes they included, made the book the effective resource it is today.

For all their hard work, their children are recognized on the next page with their adorable self-portraits.

The Illustrator: In my quest to encourage kids to find and do the things they love, it wouldn't have been right for me to use anyone other than a budding artist to design the cover and inside illustrations of my book. Enter Bryn Hobson, first year student in the Graphic Design Program at Cal Poly. After reading my book to get ideas for the cover design, he sketched a quick picture and wrote: *I plan to make the figures and text out of construction paper and use primary colors that are bold and reminiscent of childhood simplicity. Together I feel that the construction paper and primary color scheme work to convey a sense of building a young life – that is, raising a child.* His final product, gracing the cover of this book, captures the essence of my written words and brings the book's theme to life.

The Title: After hearing the theme to my book, my sister Nicole, in her thoughtful and reflective style, came up with three words that summed it up, *Raised for Richness*. And so was born the title to this book.

The Magician: For the many times he had to edit and re-edit the writing, re-format all the illustrations, and otherwise work his magical computer skills, I bow down to my awesome husband whose patience is the real reason this book is finished.

The *Raised for Richness* Kids:

Table of Contents

Introduction

Kids keep us pretty busy and, as parents, we really wouldn't have it any other way. Remember watching them take their first step, and then what seemed like only days later, whisking away on their bike? Now it's birthday parties and summer camps. And, of course, the school projects, music recitals, and back-to-school nights. Pretty soon, without warning, our "kids" will get their driver's licenses, have their first dates, and begin packing for college. There's a whirlwind of activity happening as we raise our children who seem to grow up faster by the day. And somewhere in that crazy whirlwind, we manage to squeeze in lessons on please and thank you, sharing, and financial literacy.

Uh, wait a minute. Did you say 'financial literacy'? Isn't that stuff about money...like budgets and investments? Aren't our kids a little young to be learning things like that? And, anyway, isn't that taught in schools?

It's true, financial literacy is not something we typically think of when we go down our list of things to teach our young kids. For a lot of parents, it's because they're not sure what happens after the piggy bank. For others, it's not feeling comfortable or qualified to teach their kids about money. And some parents are waiting for their kids to enter high school and get their first job before diving into budgets. But reaching kids when they are young and when their habits are forming is the best time to teach them financial literacy.

So what is financial literacy, anyway? At its simplest, financial literacy is the ability to effectively and comfortably deal with issues relating to money. And issues relating to money come up a lot. Even with kids. Um...especially with kids. Think about the latest fad at school that your child simply had to be a part of. Or the arcade games at the pizza parlor calling to your child to drop in quarter after quarter. Those are the perfect opportunities to teach your kids lessons about money. They'll learn about making good spending choices, living within their means, and they can even begin setting personal financial goals. You'd be setting the stage for the financial challenges and opportunities that await them in adulthood.

And that's very cool because, it turns out, you are your child's biggest influence when it comes to what they know about handling money. Yup, you. And the work you do with them now is very important. Consider this: in a Charles Schwab 2009 *Young Adults and Money* survey, the young adults surveyed indicated that they did not feel adequately prepared to deal with issues relating to using debt wisely, saving for the future, or investing. Their number one and number two requests when it came to learning more about money: knowing how to live within a budget and the importance of saving.

Uh oh. A lot of bad things can happen to kids when they get out there in the world and don't know how to manage money. And if you think about it, money affects just about every part of our lives from the things we can do and have to our sense of security and even our relationships. So teaching them the skills they will need to make good financial decisions is pretty important.

But how do we teach our kids those skills? How do we move beyond the piggy bank to budgeting, saving, earning, spending wisely, investing, and all the other things they need to learn about money? It starts by putting money into their hands on a regular basis. If the goal is to teach kids how to effectively manage money, then it makes sense that they have money to manage. We don't hand our teenagers the keys to the family car once they turn sixteen unless they've had practice behind the wheel first. Lots and lots of practice. It's no different with money.

I've been teaching and designing curriculum for elementary and middle school kids for over 22 years. In those years, I've learned that the best lessons are done in the context of things that are interesting, meaningful, and relevant to their lives. Kids like it when it's all about them! And the good news is, they learn better that way. So I wrote this book with that in mind. Tying the lessons and activities into their interests, this book will serve as your guide as you set up a money management system tailored to your family's individual needs. You'll learn how to teach your kids things like budgeting and setting financial goals. And because you (and your kids!) are busy people, I also designed the lessons and activities to be quick and easy to use.

Although written as a book about teaching kids money, a very special thing will happen as you work your way along the road to riches. You'll discover that talking with your kids about money often leads to discussions about what your kids want to be when they grow up…and the positive power that sharing can have…and what their favorite thing to do is (hey, that can lead to a great, happy career). Your kids will begin to reflect on their interests and desires, and they'll begin setting personal goals. They'll start to pay attention to things that motivate them and hone in on who they are as individuals. They'll discover that money is simply a tool to help them do and have the things they want; it's not an end in itself. And they'll come to understand that the really important things in life aren't things at all.

So as you begin to teach your children the ins and outs of financial literacy, know that you are equipping them with the knowledge and understanding not only about money, but about themselves as well, in order to live fulfilled, happy, and financially secure lives.

Wishing you success as you raise your children to become rich…in friends, compassion, knowledge, happiness, and, yes, money.

~ Karyn

The Book's Format

Reading the Chapters

Raised for Richness was designed so that once you've read the first chapter you are free to skip around through the other chapters. That first chapter sets the foundation for all the work done in the rest of the book.

 Chew on This Family Discussions

Here's a tidbit that's uber important. Families that share dinner together on a regular basis tend to have kids who are healthier, less stressed, have higher self-esteem, and do better academically than those who are more solitary.[1] It doesn't take much to have a huge impact.

Here's something else that's important. Parents who have regular conversations with their kids about money help their kids gain the skills and confidence they will need to handle adult financial decisions.

So I'm going to tie the two together through *Chew on This* dinner discussions. While you're sitting together as a family bonding over spaghetti and meatballs, you'll have the opportunity to discuss very important money matters with your kids. Over time, and with your guidance, your kids will learn the ins and outs of being effective money managers. And they'll probably learn a little about themselves and you, as well!

Since this book covers the ages 6 – 16, you'll need to judge the length and depth of the conversations by the interest and developmental level of your child. These dinner discussions are meant to happen over a long period of time so don't think you need to get through all the questions in one sitting. But before you know it, talking about money will be a healthy habit that has become a natural part of your everyday life.

---

1   Duke, M.P., et al. "Of Ketchup and Kin: Dinnertime Conversations as a Major Source of Family Knowledge, Family Adjustment and Family resilience." Working paper #26. Emory Center for Myth and Ritual in American Life, 2003.

Activities

Throughout the book are hands-on activities for you to do with your child to underscore the money message presented. Kids love to be actively involved in their learning and it's one of the best ways for them to retain the information.

Worksheets

Some of the discussions and activities come with worksheets. To download extras visit: http://www.kidnexions.com/RaisedforRichness/worksheets/main.htm

 My Money Reflections

At the end of each chapter you'll find *My Money Reflections*. These are questions that will allow you to think about the concepts and activities presented throughout the chapter. They also serve as a guide to help you as you work with your child.

Chapter 1:

. . .

The Foundation

*"What would you dream for if you
knew you couldn't fail?" Schuller*

My Money Experiences

Did you know that most kids learn about managing money from you, their parents, whether or not you've made an attempt to teach them? Kids are great observers; it's how they learn. Since YOU have the greatest impact on what your kids learn about money it's important that you reflect on your "money attitude" as you begin to take on the responsibility of preparing your kids for their financial futures.

Stop and reflect on your thoughts and experiences with money growing up. Use the *My Money Thoughts* worksheet as your guide.

My Money Thoughts

What is your attitude towards money? Is money a good thing, a bad thing, an annoyance, something to be avoided, an obsession?

Why do you think you have this attitude? Are you happy with feeling this way?

What attitude towards money are your kids observing in you?

Think back on growing up as a kid. What were you taught about money?

Now ask yourself: …when I left home was I prepared to manage money (budget, save, spend, invest, borrow) effectively on my own? Write down specific examples of managing money well or not-so-well.

Give some thought to how you want your kids to manage money as an adult.

If you were not prepared to manage money when you left home, what are you doing differently to make sure your kids are prepared?

What are the things you want to begin doing with your kids to help them learn to handle money effectively?

Chew on This: My Growing Up Money Experiences

Kids absolutely love to hear stories about you when you were a kid. This is an opportunity to chat with them about your money experiences growing up. You may even discover new things about your spouse, or maybe about yourself!

- Describe what you were taught about money as a kid.

- When you received money, what did you typically do with it?

- Did you have a savings account? If so, at what age did you open it?

- When you left home were you prepared to manage money (budget, save, spend, invest, borrow) effectively on your own?

- Give specific examples of managing money well and not-so-well.

- Do you wish you were taught differently about money? In what way?

- Describe how you would like your kids to manage money as an adult.

- Describe the things you want to begin doing with your kids to help them learn to handle money effectively. (You may need to read a little more of this book to get some ideas.)

My Money Values

Although just about every kid would say that they would like to be rich, let's get kids to reflect first on prioritizing what they want to be rich in. Most of us automatically think about being rich in money. But what about being rich in friends, compassion, generosity, knowledge, responsibility, enjoyment… These tie in with our values. It's okay to be rich in money, but if we aren't rich in the other things first, having all the money in the world won't help our kids lead fulfilling lives.

And how does generosity, responsibility, and enjoyment tie in with money? These values are reflected in the ways in which we choose to spend and save our money. We teach generosity when we share with those less fortunate than us. We teach responsibility and delayed gratification when we put a little of our money aside for the future. And when we splurge every once in a while on a fancy dinner out, we teach that it's good to enjoy, as well.

Conversely, shopping impulsively teaches kids that the value of a dollar is not important. Not to mention the messages sent about lack of self-discipline. And holding too tightly onto money teaches kids that more money is better at the expense of experiencing life.

If we can get our kids to be rich in the things that are important in life and then they become rich in money, just think of the fulfilling life they will lead, not to mention the impact they will have on the world.

Chew on This: My Money Values

Use the questions below as a guide to help your child reflect on the things that are really important in life. Keep in mind that wanting to be rich in money is not a bad thing. It's just a matter of setting priorities.

(Optional) Have your tweens and teens complete the *My Money Values* worksheet.

- What does it mean to value something?

- What are some things you do with our family that you value? How much do these cost?

- Name some things, besides money, that you'd like to be rich in.

- Why is it important to be rich in these other things before being rich in money? Does it really matter?

- What kinds of things can you do that would show that you value being rich in compassion, friends, etc?

- What kinds of things can you buy that would show that you value being rich in compassion, friends, etc?

- Is it okay to want to be rich in money?

- Is money good or bad? (Neither, it's a tool to help us get and do the things we need and want.)

- How can the ways we spend our money help us show what we value?

- What would you do if you won a $500 raffle prize? (If your answer included giving some of it away, it's important to be specific – who/ what organization would you give it to?)

My Money Values

List the things that are important in your life. These are things you value.

If you could spend money on anything you want, what would you buy? (You can list more than one thing.)

How do the things you would spend money on relate to the things you value? (Ex: if 'family' is one of your values and a video game is what you would buy, then sharing that game with your family ties the two together.)

How can money help us show what we value?

What would you like to be rich in?

My Look Into the Future

Just like the Cheshire cat in Alice in Wonderland told Alice when she asked which road she should take, "Well that all depends on where you want to go," we need to ask ourselves where our destination is. And we need to help our kids figure out theirs, as well. That doesn't mean that by six years old, their entire future needs to be mapped out. Things will change over time. But it's no accident that those who have a plan have a better chance of accomplishing what they set out to do. That's because when they're confronted with choices, they know their goals and make their decisions based on them.

Chew on This: My Look Into the Future

Use the questions below as a guide to help your kids visualize their future. Visualizing allows us to create specific images in our mind that can help us achieve our goals. Besides, if you never give specific thought to what you want, there's a good chance you won't get it. Athletes often use the power of visualization to help them perform better.

In addition, getting kids to reflect on their future helps them understand that the choices they make today can impact their future. Later in the book, we'll have kids take this one step further by having them come up with their *Money Game Plan*.

After you've discussed the questions have or help them fill in the information on the *My Look into the Future* worksheet. It's fun to do this every year to capture their changing thoughts. It's also a great memoir to add to your child's memory box as they get to see how their thinking changes over the years.

- Do you have some ideas about what you want to be when you grow up?

- Where do you think you might want to live? (geographic location)

- Will you live in a house or an apartment?

- If you want to live in a house, will you own the house?

- Describe the kinds of things will you have. (car, "toys", etc.)

- Describe the kinds of thing you want to do when you grow up? (travel, etc.)

- What kinds of friends will you have? (caring, understanding, respectful, etc.)

- Do you plan on having any pets?

- Do you plan on getting married and having kids?

- What kind of things motivate you?

- What role does money play in all of this?

- Why would knowing how to manage money be important to your future?

- What kind of job would you need to have to support the things you want to do and have?

- Does the answer to the above question tie in with what you want to "be" when you grow up? If not, how might you be able to turn your interests into a job that can support the things you want to have? Or, how can you manage your money now so that you can still have the things you want but be the thing you want to be?

- What do you think education has to do with the amount of money you can earn?

My L👀K Into the Future

Give a little thought to what your life will look like in the future. Use the questions from *Chew on This* to help guide your answers.

Right now I am _____ years old. In 5 years I will be _____ years old. Here is how I see my life in five years:

In 10 years I will be _____ years old. Here is how I see my life in ten years:

In 20 years I will be _____ years old. Here is how I see my life in twenty years:

Chew on This: Goal Setting

It's nice to have an idea of where we want to be in five or ten years, but how we get there depends on our goals for today, tomorrow, and next week. Kids need to learn how to set short-term goals because it's the achievement of hundreds of these short-term goals that will allow them to live in the future they envision.

- Describe a goal you have set and achieved. (I finished my Indian project on time; I learned to play the guitar, I saved $100, etc.)

- How does it make you feel to know that you can accomplish something you set out to do?

- Have you ever set a goal and not achieved it? What happened? How did that make you feel? What would you do differently next time?

- What are your specific goals for this week? (To turn in my homework on time; to finish my letter to Grannie, etc.)

- What are your specific goals for the year? (To get a part-time job; to make the cross country team, etc.)

- How do you think goals are accomplished? (You need a clear plan.)

Activity: My Short- and Long-Term Goals

Successful people know what their short- and long-term goals are. They even write them down. And since we want our kids to be successful in whatever they choose to do, we're going to teach them how to think about and write down their goals, as well.

Begin by helping your child think of her short- then her long term goals. Write these down on the *My Short- and Long-Term Goals* worksheet. Place the worksheet somewhere where she can see it every day. Periodically check in with her and ask about her progress. You may want to use the visualization exercise below to help with some of her goals.

In addition to working towards reaching their personal goals, it's also important to teach our kids to support each other's goals. Our lives become more enriched and fulfilled when we help others reach their dreams.

 Actvity: Visualization

Visualization is such an important skill for kids to learn that I'm going to spend a little more time discussing it. Teaching kids to visualize teaches them to focus on the specifics of what they want and think about the steps necessary in order to get it.

You did an activity earlier that got your kids to think about their future through visualization. It's time to bring them a little closer to the moment and get them to visualize their immediate goals. For example, do they have a soccer game or cross country meet coming up? Visualizing how they want to perform can actually help improve how they play.

In a quiet room, have them close their eyes and picture themselves on the field or on the course. Have them visualize themselves making the perfect plays or running the perfect race. They need to *see* it the way they want it done. They need to *feel* it the way they would feel it as if they were really there.

For young kids, you may want to have them visualize your words: *You're playing forward and the ball has just been hit to you. You see it rolling very quickly in your direction. You glance at the goal and notice an opening. Your foot catches the ball and you begin dribbling towards the goal. You can feel yourself breathing heavy, then you see that opening. In one quick motion, you kick the ball as hard as you can. You watch it sail past two defenders and right into the goal net. Then all you hear are cheers from your teammates as they come to slap you on the back.*

You can do this with other areas of their lives as well. How about a goal to save $100 in two months? Have them visualize doing some above-and-beyond jobs (described in Chapter 5) to earn the money. Then have them visualize placing money in an envelope or watching the balance in their account grow. How does watching that pile of money grow make them feel? If they're saving the $100 to purchase an item, have them visualize being at the store, choosing the item, paying for it, taking it home and opening it, etc.

My Short- and Long-Term Goals

These are my short-term goals (include the date you want to reach the goal):	These are the reasons for my goal:				These are the steps to help me reach my goal:				

These are my long-term goals (include the date you want to reach the goal):	These are the reasons for my goal:				These are the steps to help me reach my goal:				

Money Personalities

Some of us are morning people, others are night owls. Some like to swim, others would rather sit by the pool. We all have different personalities. The more we know about our personality, the easier it is to enhance the good stuff and work on the not-so-good.

The same is true of our money personalities. Some of us are savers while others are spenders. Some balance their checkbook to the penny each month while others have two checking accounts so they never have to balance any checkbook. (I had a roommate like that. No kidding.) The better understanding we have of our individual money personality, the easier it is to come up with strategies to help balance us out and, ultimately, make us better money managers.

 Chew on This: Money Personalities

This is a fun activity to do with tweens and teens. Read *My Money Personalities* below and discuss with your child the pluses and minuses of each personality. Then use the descriptions to help figure out which money personalities you and your child lean toward keeping in mind that you may lean towards several. Follow up with the accompanying strategies to talk about ways to help balance out the personalities.

Are you a worrier? *The worrier is always fretting about money. Do I have any? Is it enough? What happens if I stop getting money? If I spend this money will I start spending all my money?*

Strategies to overcome constantly worrying about money: Come up with a spending and saving plan and write it down. Worriers often need to see their strategy before they believe it will work. Decide on a percentage of the allowance that will go towards long-term saving (investing money), short-term saving (saving to spend on something specific in the next several weeks or months), sharing, and spending (money that they can spend worry-free).

Are you a carefree spender? *Carefree spenders loves shopping. They love having the latest fads. Their self-control in the midst of a mall evaporates. They don't really worry about where the money is going to come from. Credit cards are their friends.*

Strategies for overcoming spending too much: Put tweens and teens in charge of **all** their spending for a given month. This includes toiletries, entertainment, school lunches, etc. Give them their budget in cash. They need to see the money being spent. If they blow all their money on unnecessary items, they're stuck until the next month rolls around.

If your child is younger than a tween, do the same but do it on a weekly basis.

Are you a penny pincher? *Penny pinchers aren't worried about money. They simply won't spend any. They don't mind missing out on opportunities if it means they get to keep their money. They're not a lot of fun to be around where money is concerned.*

Strategies for overcoming penny pinching tendencies: Have your child put aside a certain percentage of his income. Then help him decide what he can spend it on. Let him know that if he can't come up with anything, it will be donated to charity.

Once he's spent the money, talk to him about all the wonderful things that happened as a result of his letting go. *How wonderful that you bought that video game. You and your sister have really enjoyed playing it together. I'm glad you decided to let go of some of your money.*

Are you a giver? *Givers are generous people. And if they have a lot of money to spare, their generosity can have a big impact on the world.*

Then there are those who give who perhaps aren't in the best financial position to share all their money. At face value it seems nice but if we don't teach these givers to take care of their needs first, they may find themselves in a position of becoming dependent on others.

Strategies for teaching givers to meet their needs first: We need to teach givers to *pay themselves first*. Every time they receive money, a percentage automatically goes into savings. Then remind them periodically how nice it is that they have that extra money for unexpected things that come up or perhaps a goal they have set. We want them to develop the same warm fuzzies they get when they see their personal savings grow as when they give their money away. Over time, they will learn the value of paying themselves first.

Are you a saver? *Savers seem to naturally see the benefit of putting money aside. They usually display strong self-discipline traits. When they discover all the different ways their saved money can make even more money, they get giddy. They do have to be careful, though, that they don't get carried away with saving and enter the penny pinching category.*

Strategies for keeping a saver from crossing into the penny pinching category: Applaud their decision to buy such-and-such and give the reasons why it was a good choice.

Are you disinterested in money? *There will most definitely be kids who are simply not interested in anything money related. Depending on their age, that's okay. Your job will be to continually guide them to manage money following the steps outlined in this book. As kids enter the teenage years, however, it will become more important to address this head-on as we want to establish healthy habits while they are still living with you.*

As adults not having addressed these issues, the disinterested turn into avoiders. Avoiders don't like paying bills or balancing a checkbook. They certainly have not considered a budget. They spend money and hope for the best. We do not want this for our kids.

Strategies for helping the disinterested become a little more responsible with money: You're going to have to play a bigger role than usual to get the disinterested to understand and learn how to effectively deal with money. And it's important that they complete the hands-on work described in this book. If necessary, offer little incentives to complete the activities such as extra computer time or whatever things or activities motivate your child. They will, at the very least, have the skills to take with them into adulthood.

Are you unaware? *Unaware spenders don't seem to realize that how they spend money affects the lifestyle choices they have. They haven't given any thought* *to making a budget. And although they may live within their means, they aren't preparing themselves for their financial future.*

Strategies for reflecting more on money: Often it's simply a matter of showing them all the different things they can do with their money: save, invest, share. When they realize they have choices with their money, they usually begin to make adjustments to their habits.

My Money Reflections — The Money Foundation

Think about the lessons in this chapter and answer the following questions:

☐ I understand the significant role I play in helping prepare my child for his financial future.

☐ I will make a concerted effort to bring everyone together for a family dinner several times a week. This alone can contribute to healthier, more academically focused, and more confident kids.

☐ I have thought about my attitude towards money and plan on making a conscious effort to change the areas I'm not happy with.

☐ I have thought about what I learned as a child about money and I know the things I would do the same for my kids as well as the things I would change.

☐ I have discussed with my child that it's important to be rich in friends, compassion, knowledge, understanding, etc. before they become rich in money.

☐ My tween/teen has thought about her future aspirations and has a general idea of her direction. She understands that in order to accomplish her goals she will need to learn how to effectively manage money.

☐ My child has written down his short- and long-term goals and has a plan to help him achieve his goals.

☐ I have taught my child how to visualize one of her goals.

☐ I have talked to my kids about the importance of supporting each other's goals.

☐ I have talked about different money personalities with my tween/teen. We know the strengths of each and will practice the strategies to work on the weaknesses.

Chapter 2:

. . .

Allowance

"The greatest thing you can give your children are the roots of responsibility and the wings of independence." Denis Waitley

The best way to teach kids how to manage money is by putting money into their hands on a regular basis. The most popular way to do this is through an allowance program. Giving your child an allowance is one of the most effective tools we have to teach them how to manage *their* money. After all, if the goal is to get our kids to be great money managers, and it is, then they're going to need money to manage. And, until your kids are old enough to get a part-time job, an allowance is the way to go. Consider it an investment in your child's future.

An allowance gives your child the opportunity to *do* money. Doing money involves learning how to budget, set personal financial goals, spend wisely, save, share, borrow, earn, and invest. We need to teach these skills from an early age if we want our kids to grow up prepared to handle adult financial decisions. A good time to start an allowance program is when your child enters her "formal" years of schooling, around age five or six.

Once your child starts receiving an allowance, consider it her salary for learning how to effectively manage money. That means it's going to need to be paid on time and consistently. You probably wouldn't feel so great if your employer was flaky about getting you your paycheck. After all, you make a lot of financial decisions based on knowing when your paycheck is coming in. The same should be true for your child. If she is working towards a purchase, then she needs to be able to rely on consistent paydays. And even if she doesn't have a personal financial goal in mind, it's important to show her that you value her money enough to make sure she gets it on time.

A great way to automate allowance is through a kids' savings and money management software program called KidsSave (www.kidnexions.com). The nice thing about automating allowance via the computer is that it's a great way to be consistent about giving allowance and it's harder for your kids to spend money they don't have easy access to!

A Shifting of Responsibility

Another way to look at an allowance program is as a shifting of responsibility. Instead of you paying for all of your child's discretionary items, let him do it. And allowing him to make his own choices is going to help teach the difference between needs and wants. That's because when it's his money on the line, the difference between needs and wants takes on a whole new meaning. You'd be surprised how stingy he can become with *his* money.

The nice thing is, you're not putting out extra money. You're just letting him handle the spending decisions. And here's a huge added bonus. No more power struggles! If he wants something while you're out shopping, great. If he has the money, let him get it. If he doesn't, then he's going to have to save up. That's it. End of discussion.

Teaching Kids How to Make Decisions

As mentioned above, the key to an effective allowance program is to give your kids personal control over what happens to their money. To do this, you're going to need to relinquish some control. Not all control. There are certainly some definite 'Nos' when it comes to spending money. And there are rules, such as when it's an appropriate time to eat the candy they just bought. Just because they can buy their own stuff doesn't make it a free-for-all.

But for the most part, you need to let your child learn how to make good decisions. This comes through trial and error. Even though it may drive you crazy to see your child spend money on something you just know is a poor choice, it's important for her to experience the consequence. Then talk to her about how she could do it differently next time. Kids don't often know how to problem solve so it's up to us to help guide them. And keep in mind that something we parents may think is a mistake to spend money on, just may turn out to be the item-of-the-year for your child.

A note about making mistakes: Mistakes are one of the most powerful teaching tools we have. Although they can be annoying, frustrating, and sometimes even embarrassing, if we take the time to help our kids learn from their mistakes, we are giving them a skill that will carry them through their entire lives. So instead of looking at mistakes as having done something wrong, help your child look at them as great learning opportunities. And then, when it comes to the really, really important choices, they will have the skills to reflect first, then choose.

The Allowance/Chore Debate

Should you tie allowance to completing chores? There are great arguments on both sides of this issue. I'm going to land in the center and take the best of both.

No. Don't tie chores and allowance: Those in this camp feel that paying kids to do things they should do anyway as being a part of a family teaches kids that there is a price tag for everything. They also feel that if we tie allowance to whether or not chores are completed, we run the risk of them not completing their chores. If they don't do their chores, they don't get money and then can't learn how to manage it. And, finally, what happens when kids are old enough to get a job? Do they still get paid to make their bed?

Yes. Tie chores and allowance: Those in this camp feel that kids need to learn that in the real world money is earned. They feel that giving kids money for nothing teaches a sense of entitlement.

The best of both: We're going to teach our kids that there are certain responsibilities they have by default of being a family member. No-one is going to pay them to keep their dorm room clean or to wash their utensils in the office kitchen when they're older.

Then we're going to set up an allowance system so that they will receive money on a regular basis. It's not money-for-nothing, though. Their job will be to learn how to manage it responsibly according to the "rules" you set up with your child. More on this when we discuss the Allowance Program coming up.

And, finally, because what they will be getting for allowance will not cover that ipod or cell phone they want, they will be given opportunities to learn how to earn money through extra jobs that you set up. We'll cover this in greater detail in Chapter 5.

How Much? How Often?

A good rule of thumb for how much allowance a child should receive per week is half your child's age per week. So following this rule, if you have a seven-year-old, he would receive $3.50 weekly allowance.

Using this as a starting point, there are other things to consider as well, such as what your budget can afford and your expectations for how the allowance is to be used. In other words, does your child need to pull out a certain amount for tithing or long-term savings? Will he be paying for school lunches? As expectations rise so will the amount. But don't give him so much that he never "feels the pinch". We want kids to learn how to earn money as well. Again, we'll cover that in Chapter 5.

Once the expectations for the allowance are decided, adjust the allowance accordingly. It is typical for teenagers to receive at least their age in allowance per week. In addition, to give teens practice in budgeting you may consider giving them the allowance bi-weekly or even monthly.

The following table gives a general outline of some possible expenses your child should become responsible for:

6-8 year olds weekly allowance	9-12 year olds weekly allowance	13+ year olds bi-weekly or monthly allowance
• bubble gum/candy • trading cards • extra toys/stuffed animals	• all of the previous expenses plus... • movies with friends • video games/CDs/ itunes	• all of the previous expenses plus... • cell phone bill* • toiletries/haircuts and supplies • entertainment • gifts *can be all or a portion of the bill

Track Expenses

If you're still not convinced about giving your child an allowance, do this simple activity. Help your child track expenses for at least two weeks. Use the *Daily Income and Expenses Tracking Worksheet* to record all extra items your child buys (I paid) or that you buy for him (Someone else paid). These could be a slurpee at the mall, a new binder, or a stuffed animal. You may be surprised at just how quickly it all adds up.

Now, think about not having to deal with making those purchases. Instead, the responsibility becomes your child's. She'll be learning real life skills through managing money that would have been spent anyway. Remember, if we want to teach responsibility we have to give responsibility. In addition, and really the best part, it will eliminate the constant *mom, can I have* syndrome.

Daily Income and Expenses Tracking Worksheet

Date	Item	Income	Expenses	Need	Want	I paid	Someone else paid
		$	$				
		$	$				
		$	$				
		$	$				
		$	$				
		$	$				
		$	$				
		$	$				
		$	$				
		$	$				
		$	$				
		$	$				
		$	$				
		$	$				
		$	$				

The Allowance Program

Along with an allowance comes responsibility. Remember, the point of giving an allowance is to teach kids how to effectively manage money. When kids have the skills to effectively manage their money, they have options. And it's these options that can play a significant role in living the life they ultimately want.

Chew on This: Allowance and Responsibilities

Here is a starter list of responsibilities that comes with an allowance. Discuss these with your child before you begin the program. Then fill out the *Allowance Contract* to set up clear and consistent rules and expectations for both you and your child.

- Learning to make good choices

- Understanding you are responsible for all your discretionary spending

- Understanding that there are no advances on allowance (when the money is gone, it's gone)

- Learning from your money mistakes

- Keeping money in a safe place (wallet, piggy bank, real bank, etc.)

- Learning to save

- Learning to share

- Learning money equivalents (10 dimes = one dollar)

- No borrowing (until late teens)

- Keeping track of spending

- Prioritizing spending

- Learning how to create and achieve personal financial goals

Dividing Income Into Categories

Most kids think the only thing that can be done with money is to spend it. We need to teach them that we actually have choices with our money. Those include short- and long-term savings, giving, and investing.

Split the Money: Whether or not you require your kids to allocate a certain amount of their income into individual categories is up to you. Some families like to have their kids put 10% towards saving, 10% towards sharing, and the rest in their spending (short-term savings) category. Some families split the percentages differently and may include an investing, or some other, category. You'll need to decide what works best for you. A good, visual way for young kids to see their money divided into categories is to label jars with the category name and the percentage allocated for that category.

Don't Split the Money: Then there are those families that don't require that their kids split any money, at all. It all ends up in one big pot where the kids will learn over time the benefits of saving, investing, and sharing. These families believe that their kids need to learn these benefits on their own. When their child doesn't have enough money to buy the video game he wants because he spent it all on dollar-toys, these parents step in and remind him that if he had saved some of his money, he might have enough to buy the game. Suggesting that he start putting money aside for savings but allowing him to make the decision let's him be in charge of his money. Since saving money is such an important habit for kids to get into, in Chapter 4 we'll cover some incentives to jumpstart kids into the habit of saving.

Gift Money: You'll also need to consider what happens to gift money. Although it's tempting to want to have your child divide the money into categories, think about it in terms of any other gift she would receive. We don't have her split the new ballet shoes she received as a gift into categories. So why would it be any different if the gift comes in the form of dollar bills? It should all go into her spending category so that she can buy herself the gift she wants.

That said, sometimes grandma and grandpa get pretty generous. Talk with your child about putting some of that money into long-term savings making sure she still has enough to go out and buy herself something nice.

Earning Extra Money

There are certain responsibilities that kids have by default of being a family member. They come in the form of setting the table, taking out the garbage, and making our beds. We do not pay kids for these.

There should, however, be ways for kids to earn additional money by being able to choose from a variety of household jobs. These could include mowing the lawn, washing the car, and pulling weeds. An allowance should give kids just enough to cover most of their weekly expenses but not enough to allow them to do and have all the things they want. So these extra jobs offer kids an opportunity to *earn* extra money. We'll discuss this in greater detail in Chapter 5.

We get the best of both worlds this way: kids who learn not to expect a hand-out for everything they do but who also learn that if they need additional money, it's going to take some work.

 Tween/Teen Activity: Negotiating an Allowance/Raise

Kids negotiate all the time. *Mom, can I have this candy? I promise I'll still eat all my dinner. Dad, can I spend the night at Justin's? You don't have to worry about me being tired tomorrow because his mom always makes us go to bed early.*

Their negotiations are usually on the fly and sometimes they "win" and sometimes they don't. But since kids are going to be negotiating the rest of their lives and these negotiations are going to become increasingly more important (think: re-do of a school assignment or a raise in wages), let's give them practice in the skills of being an effective negotiator. For this exercise we're going to teach kids to effectively negotiate an allowance or, if they already have an allowance, a raise in their allowance.

Go over the *My Allowance Negotiation/My Raise Negotiation* information on the next page. Then have them come up with and write down supporting reasons for their request on the worksheet. You may need to role-play with them if there is no-one else to do it. That's okay. They will probably learn a lot more about the way you think with you "playing" their parent! Then let them make an appointment to meet with you to discuss their request.

Although kids really do negotiate all the time, this is probably the first "formal" negotiation they've done. They might be nervous so try to make them feel comfortable. Offer them a lemonade or hot chocolate. Remember, this is awesome practice for real life; we want them to be relaxed. Of course, don't feel like you need to give in to all their requests, but do give them a chance. You may need to compromise just like they might need to. Keep in mind the phrase: *If you want to teach responsibility, you have to give responsibility.*

Good luck to both sides!

My Allowance Negotiation/My Raise Negotiation

How to be an effective negotiator: People negotiate when they want something from someone else. Some people are afraid to negotiate because they look at it as a confrontation. A negotiation is not a confrontation, unless you make it one. So the first lesson is: your attitude. Always go into a negotiation with respect for the other person and the other person's position.

Next, be prepared. That means that you're going to need to have a clear idea of what you want and the reasons you want it. Write these down below. But keep in mind that even though you can justify your requests, your parents may not agree with everything you say. Know that you may need to compromise. Compromising is not a bad thing and it helps everyone walk away from the table feeling like they got something.

When you've got your list ready, find someone to role-play with. Being able to effectively communicate your message is important and that only happens if you've practiced what you intend to say. Maybe you can even have this person take the opposite side so that you get practice answering questions your parents may come up with.

Finally, a good negotiator is also a good listener. If you don't listen to the other person's point of view, you are not showing respect for them. It doesn't mean you have to agree with them, but you do need to listen and take their arguments into consideration. This is when compromise may be the best solution.

When you feel like you're prepared, set up an appointment. Yes, that's right. Parents are busy people and this is an important discussion. Show them how mature you are becoming by taking their time into consideration. And then, when it's time to meet, know that you have what it takes to be able to negotiate with confidence.

My Allowance Negotiation/My Raise Negotiation - Sample

Sample answers for negotiating an allowance:

- I will now be responsible for paying for all my wants.

- Receiving an allowance will give me practice in managing money.

- I will learn how to make good choices.

- I will be ready to handle money decisions when I leave home.

- I will make sure school always comes first and will always try my hardest.

- I will no longer bother you for any money.

- I will save some of my money for my long-term goals.

- I will save $200 and then begin learning how to invest my money to make it work for me.

- I will keep track of all my expenses.

- I will learn how to budget.

Sample answers for negotiating a raise:

- The things I am now buying are much more expensive.

- I have proved that I am responsible with money.

- I do my research before spending any money.

- I am a year older and have more responsibilities.

- I have added more things to the list of things I pay for such as gas, haircuts, etc.

- I do above-and-beyond jobs but it's still not enough to cover all my expenses.

My Allowance Negotiation/My Raise Negotiation

List below the reasons that support your desire for an allowance or raise:

Allowance Contract

Giving kids an allowance and then putting them in charge of making decisions about how to spend, save, share, and invest their money is a great way to teach kids hands-on lessons in money management.

Have a discussion with your child about the responsibility that comes with an allowance then fill in the following together. It's a good idea to review the contract yearly as allowance and responsibilities increase.

0 These are the things I will be responsible for paying for with my allowance (example, clothing, entertainment, lunches, etc.):

0 Based on the list above, my allowance will be $_____ weekly/biweekly/ monthly (circle one).

0 My allowance will be paid on _____ (day of week or time of month).

0 This is where I will keep my money:

0 (optional) This is how I will divide my allowance into categories: (example: 10% saving, 10% sharing, 10% investing, 70% spending)

Child signature: _____ Date: _____

Parent/guardian signature: _____ Date: _____

Advances

A part of teaching kids how to budget and live within their means is to have them experience that when the money is gone, it's gone. Until the next pay cycle. Research shows that 40% of parents who give their kids an allowance say that their child runs out of money before the next pay day. And most of these parents end up succumbing and handing over more money. Kids say that when they "borrow" money from their parents, most of their parents end up forgetting about the owed money. And the cycle continues. That's not the lesson we want our kids to learn.

So don't do it! It's important, very important, that our kids learn that when the money is gone, it really is gone. There will be a time to teach them about loans and interest. But right now it's all about teaching them to make good choices. Don't deny your kids the opportunity to learn this life lesson. And really, why can't they do a few extra jobs to earn the extra money? (Give them the money AFTER they do the work!)

Loans and Interest

It didn't take long for me to get from *don't loan money to your child* to *this is how you loan money to your child*. The key is to never loan money until you know your child has absorbed the lesson that when the money is gone it is gone. They've proven they can make good spending choices and they've set and achieved personal financial goals.

At this point, there may come a time when an item they so desperately want goes on sale and, being good consumers, they just can't pass up the opportunity. That's when you loan them the money – with interest. Set up a payment plan and make sure they can see the difference between what the item cost and how much they will end up paying in total due to interest. Instead of amortizing the interest, the easiest way to do this is to simply calculate interest on the cost of the item and add the cost plus interest together to get the final total cost.

Don't worry that they may not understand exactly how to calculate the interest. The important thing is that they understand the connection between borrowing and paying back more than they borrowed. In fact, having them see how much the coveted item will really cost them is always an enlightening experience. They may decide they don't like the terms of the loan and go back to good old fashioned saving.

BTW, a short-term loan such as waiting until you get home from shopping to have your child pay you back, is okay. It's not often our kids are wandering around with their wallets and purses. The important part is that they pay you upon arrival home…which means they really do have the money.

Ryan's Repayment Plan				
Video Game $50 + 10% interest = $55.00				
Week Number	Principal Payment	Interest (10%/week)	Total Payment	Balance
				$55.00
1	$5.00	$0.50	$5.50	$49.50
2	$5.00	$0.50	$5.50	$44.00
3	$5.00	$0.50	$5.50	$38.50
4	$5.00	$0.50	$5.50	$33.00
5	$5.00	$0.50	$5.50	$27.50
6	$5.00	$0.50	$5.50	$22.00
7	$5.00	$0.50	$5.50	$16.50
8	$5.00	$0.50	$5.50	$11.00
9	$5.00	$0.50	$5.50	$5.50
10	$5.00	$0.50	$5.50	$0.00

My Money Reflections – Allowance

Think about the lessons in this chapter and answer the following questions:

☐ Do I understand that in order for my child to learn how to effectively manage money, she is going to need money to manage?

☐ Have I helped my child understand the responsibilities that come with receiving an allowance?

☐ Have we agreed upon the amount of allowance he will receive and how often he will get it?

☐ Have we decided if my child will be splitting her allowance into categories and what the percentages will be?

☐ Have we decided what will happen to gift money my child receives?

☐ Does my child understand that the allowance will probably not cover all of his expenses and that there is a list of jobs he can do to earn extra money? (Discussed in depth in Chapter 5)

☐ Have I committed to my child that I will be consistent in paying out the allowance?

☐ Do I understand that it's important for me to allow my child to make her own spending choices?

☐ If my child makes a poor spending choice, can I help him come up with strategies to do things differently the next time?

☐ Does my child understand that if she asks for anything my answer will be, "Sure, you can have (fill in the blank) as long as you have the money to pay for it"?

☐ Does my child understand that I will not be giving advances in allowance?

☐ Does my child understand that when the money is gone, it is gone until the next allowance cycle?

☐ Does my child understand what a negotiator is and have we discussed ways to be an effective negotiator?

☐ Has my child set up an appointment to negotiate an allowance/raise?

☐ Did we reach an agreement during the negotiation?

☐ Have we filled in and signed the Allowance Contract?

Chapter 3:

...

Sharing

You have never really lived until
you've done something for somebody
who can never repay you.   Unknown

Let's face it. Our kids are pretty fortunate. They have food, clothing, and shelter. Their needs are met, and probably a lot of their wants. So it's important to teach our kids to give back. And it's amazing at how many unexpected things come our way when we share unconditionally. Allowing our kids to experience this is a wonderful gift.

Getting the Kids Involved

Chew on This: Making the World a Better Place

Go around the table and talk about some things to be grateful for: our health, a nice home, good food, wonderful friends... Then discuss the fact that not all kids are as lucky as your family. Depending on the ages of your kids, you may keep it simple or choose to go into greater depth about some of the reasons why.

Then tell them that it would be nice for the family to get involved in helping make the world a better place. Brainstorm ways to do this. The ideas generated may include monetary gifts as well as the gift of time or donations. If you are already making regular monetary contributions to a charity or church organization, be sure your kids are aware of the reasons why you are sharing your money and how that money is going to be used. This allows them to "see" your values in action. Remember, many of our values are imparted to our kids through the ways in which we choose to spend our money.

During your discussion, the people, places, or things that need your help may have been brought up. If not, do it now. A great place to start is with the interests of your kids. Do they like animals? What about donating dog food to an animal shelter? Are they passionate about reading? Maybe your local library could use some money to buy additional books. Or perhaps you have a child who enjoys being around other kids. Could he donate some of her time helping at the women and children's homeless shelter?

If your kids decide to donate money or a gift, a great way to show them your support of their chosen organization(s) is to match them dollar for dollar or gift for gift. Now they can really get excited about sharing because their organization will be receiving even more with your additional contribution.

Then discuss the feelings that come with sharing:

- How does it make you feel to share?

- How do you think the person/organization receiving the sharing feels?

- What would the world be like if people didn't share their time and resources with others?

Regular Sharing Allocations

Some families have their kids automatically share a percentage of their income. For example, if your child receives $5 weekly allowance, they may automatically remove 10%, or fifty cents, and put that in their "share" pile. Other families encourage their kids to share at specific times throughout the year. You decide what works best for your situation.

Chew on This: Gimme Three!

"Change your thoughts and you change your world." Norman Vincent Peale

Life is full of so many wonderful things. Sometimes we get so busy *doing* life that we forget to *live* life. This little exercise is intended to get you and your kids to reflect on the positive things that happened throughout the day. It's also a way to train your kids to think positively. Our thoughts have a huge impact on the quality of our lives. They influence our dreams and desires and impact our ability to achieve them. So establishing the healthy habit of positive thoughts can help our kids build the confidence they need to fulfill their dreams. And when people are fulfilling their dreams, they're often in a position to help others, as well.

Tell your kids that every night for the rest of their lives (well, at least while they're hanging out with you) they are going to share three positive things about the day. No kidding. You're going to do this each night. Not one week. Not one month. But forever. Well, do it as long as you can.

Begin by going around the dinner table, starting with yourself, and sharing three positive things about your day. For example, you may say, *My first thing is that I'm proud of myself for finally solving a difficult problem at work, second - I'm glad grandma and grandpa arrived home safely this afternoon, and third, it made me happy to be able to watch you run in your meet today.*

Over time, they will learn that the things that truly make a difference in our lives are not always those that can be bought. And this helps bring an important kind of richness to their lives.

A personal note: I've been doing this for over three years with my kids who are, as of this writing, 14- and 16-years old. In the beginning it took them a few minutes to come up with their *three things*. But after a while they'd say things like, "Oh, I know what one of my three things is going to be," and the day wasn't half over! They had begun looking for and reflecting on positive things in their day! And when you're thinking about positive things, there's no room for negative things. That's a bonus!

I decided to do an experiment one night and deliberately didn't ask them about their three things. I turned to walk away and my oldest said, "Hey, we haven't done our three things yet!" I was surprised at how important this little ritual had become and how quickly looking for the positives in their lives had become a habit.

My Money Reflections - Sharing

Think about the lessons in this chapter and answer the following questions:

☐ Do I have on-going discussions with my child about all the wonderful things we have to be thankful for?

☐ Have I shared with my child the different charities/organizations I contribute to and the reasons why?

☐ Have we decided as a family which organizations we will support?

☐ Does my child know how much he will be sharing with his organization?

☐ Have I decided to match my child's contributions to encourage her and show support of her chosen organization?

☐ Am I in the habit of asking my child each night to list three positive things that happened to him that day?

Chapter 4:

. . .

Saving

*"He that can have patience can
have what he will." Ben Franklin*

Saving money is hard. And for a lot of kids, it's really hard. But it's also important. Really, really important. If we want our kids to be financially secure as adults, they are going to need to be savvy in the art of saving.

Did you know that most of our habits are formed when we are young? And that trying to re-teach ourselves new, healthier habits, although not impossible, is much more difficult the older we get? That's why we need to teach our kids how to save when they are young so they can carry these positive, healthy habits with them into adulthood.

Saving money is important for obvious reasons. It allows us to get many of the things we want. And it provides us with a sense of security. But there are some other reasons to consider as well, especially when it comes to teaching our kids.

First, saving helps reinforce the idea of delayed gratification. Delaying gratification means that you're putting off spending money now for something in the future. And studies show that those who can delay gratification when they're young tend to have higher paying jobs, better relationships, and better health as adults. Don't we all want this for our kids!

Second, when unexpected things come up, like being invited to go to a theme park with their bestest buddy, it's nice for them to have the money to be able to do it…or at the very least, be able to bring spending money.

Third, through saving kids can accumulate enough money to begin investing. And it's through investing where they can set themselves up for wealth later in life.

And finally, there's nothing like the sense of satisfaction and pride that kids feel when they achieve a savings goal. This builds confidence that can seep into other parts of their lives. And confidence building in kids…well that's the icing on the cake.

It all begins with *paying yourself first*. This simply means that when your child receives money, she takes a portion of it and puts it away in her "long-term saving pile". This could be a savings account, a piggy bank, an envelope, or some other safe place. The key is to get her in the habit of automatically paying herself first…putting money aside.

But because most kids live in the here-and-now, the thought of putting money aside does not often make sense. So we need to step in and offer kids reasons to save and provide little incentives along the way until saving becomes a healthy habit. After all, if they want to own a car or home or have enough for retirement, they're going to need to have practice in not spending all their money.

Reasons to Save

Has your child ever come to you with something that he's just got to have but has no money to get it? That's the perfect opportunity for you to introduce the idea of a reason to save. Saving money can help us get the things we want. And saving for something in particular gives kids a concrete reason to save.

Kids learn to save for something by setting personal financial goals which is addressed in more detail below. There are short-term goals and there are long-term goals. Short-term goals typically go out several weeks to several months, sometimes even a year, and are usually for things like toys, video games or cell phones. Long-term goals usually involve saving for a car, investing, or college and can go out many years.

A great place for kids to save money is at a bank or credit union. It is highly recommended that you take your kids to open a savings account, if they don't already have one. Kids love to act "grown-up" and tapping into this interest may be the spark that ignites their life-long saving habit. Not to mention that it's harder to spend money they don't have easy access to!

Incentives to Save

Even if kids have a reason to save, putting money aside can still be a hard lesson to learn. To help establish this important life skill we sometimes need to give them little motivators. These motivators come in the form of matching funds and interest. KidsSave, a kids' savings and money management software program (www.kidnexions.com) can help you set these up so they are automatic.

- Matching Funds: Match their savings dollar for dollar, or quarter for dollar, or whatever fits your budget. It's like their own little 401(k) plan. What kid doesn't like free money? Okay, so it may not be free to you, but the saving habit you are establishing now could save you a lot of money later on.

- Interest: Interest from a child's bank or credit union savings account is pretty nominal. Kids typically have small balances and a small interest rate applied to a small balance doesn't amount to a whole lot. It's hard to get too excited about twelve cents, even for a kid. So give them interest on their savings by customizing the rate so that their account can grow faster. This is another example of "free" money and over time will introduce them to the power of...

- ...compound interest. Einstein calls compound interest the eighth wonder of the world. And for good reason. Over time even small amounts of money can grow into lots of money. A good way to help kids understand this is by having them "see" their money grow visually. You can use KidsSave to help illustrate how money can grow or try the yarn activity described in Chapter 8.

Not only are these great little incentives to get kids to save their money, but they have the added benefit of growing their account balances quicker which, in turn, motivates them to save even more!

If you do choose to offer incentives to encourage saving and your kids divide their money into different categories, you'll need to decide which categories receive the "reward". In other words, will you be offering the matching/interest to all their categories, ex. spending, sharing, saving, investing. Or will it be just one or two of the categories?

Chew on This: Saving Money

Open up a discussion about saving:

- How can people keep their money safe? (This may lead to a discussion on banks. Clarify any misunderstandings about how a bank works.)

- Why is it important to save money?

- Is it easy for you to save? Why or why not?

- What are the advantages of saving?

- What are the disadvantages of saving?

- What are some of the things you'd like to save for?

- Describe some things that you, the parent, have saved or are saving for. Explain how you did it.

How Much Should I Save?

Once your child is on board with the benefits of saving, you need to decide how much they will be putting aside to save each week in the form of long-term savings. A popular rule of thumb is 10% of their income. But you decide what works best for you and your kids.

Setting Personal Financial Goals

> *"Goals are dreams with dead-lines." Diana Scharf Hunt*

In 1960, a psychology researcher at Stanford named Michael Mischel, did an experiment. He offered 4-year olds marshmallows. But he told them that if they could wait to eat the marshmallow until he returned from an errand, he would give them an additional one. 1/3 ate the marshmallow right away.

1/3 waited a little while and then ate it, and 1/3 waited for the researcher to return.

Fast forward to this same group of kids as adults. Mischel found that those who resisted the temptation of the marshmallow tended to have higher incomes, successful marriages, and better health than those who ate the marshmallow. This group also demonstrated persistence, self-motivation, and the ability to delay gratification while they pursued their goals.

The implications of this study can have a profound impact on the lives of our kids. How can we help them develop the skill of delaying gratification so that they have a better chance at being successful and healthy adults? It starts with the little things. Buying a special treat at the store but waiting until after dinner (a long time for a youngster) to eat it. Or resisting the temptation to open grandma's birthday gift that just arrived in the mail until it's actually their birthday. Or waiting to be the proud owner of a cell phone until the ripe age of...13.

Setting personal financial goals is another great way to reinforce delayed gratification. And setting goals also teaches planning ahead, another important life skill. There are three types of financial goals kids can set:

- To purchase a specific item

- To reach a certain account balance

- To save a certain amount of money

The very first goal you set up with your child should be easily attainable in a relatively short period of time. This will increase the chance that she will want to set up another goal, at which point you can increase the time and amount she needs to save. And remember, sometimes goals need revamping along the way. There's nothing wrong with that as long as your child is making an attempt to achieve her goal.

Helping your child with her first goal:

- Pick a short goal, 1 - 2 weeks.

- To remind her of her goal, find or have her draw or find a picture of what she's saving for and place it in a prominent location, like the refrigerator or front of her bedroom door.

- Help her come up with the steps necessary to achieve it (See *My Savings Plan* worksheet):

    o   How much is the item? (or the amount she wants to save)

    o   How much can she save towards the goal each week? (You may need to help her figure out how much income she bring in each week and subtract her expenses.)

    o   Using the above information, how many weeks will it take for her to reach their goal?

- When she achieves his goal, celebrate her success.

- Create a longer goal and repeat.

For a quick, easy way to create goals, especially if your child receive matching funds or interest, use KidsSave.

My Savings Plan - Sample

Choose one:

☐ Item Description: _____Used Pokemon Wii_____Cost $25___

☐ Amount I Want to Save: $_____   ☐ Account Balance I Want to Reach $_____

Weekly income (includes allowance, extra money)		$ 5.00
Weekly expenses (includes charity, long-term saving, fun money)		$ 2.00
(Subtract expenses from income) Total amount available per week		$ 3.00

Week Number	Amount Earned Each Week	Projected Amount Saved Balance	Actual Amount Saved Balance
1	$3.00	$3.00	$3.00
2	$3.00	$6.00	$6.00
3	$3.00	$9.00	$8.50
4	$3.00	$12.00	$11.50
5	$3.00	$15.00	$16.50
6	$3.00	$18.00	$19.50
7	$3.00	$21.00	$22.00
8	$3.00	$24.00	$24.50
9	$3.00	$27.00	$27.50
10			

It will take me _____9_____ weeks to achieve my goal. I had _____$2.50_____ left-over.

My Savings Plan

Choose one:

☐ Item Description: _____ Cost $_____

☐ Amount I Want to Save: $_____ ☐ Account Balance I Want to Reach $_____

Weekly income (includes allowance, extra money)	$
Weekly expenses (includes charity, long-term saving, fun money)	$
(Subtract expenses from income) Total amount available per week	$

Week Number	Amount Earned Each Week	Projected Amount Saved Balance	Actual Amount Saved Balance
1			
2			
3			
4			
5			
6			
7			
8			
9			
10			

It will take me _____ weeks to achieve my goal. I had _____ left-over.

My Money Reflections – Saving

Think about the activities in this chapter and answer the following questions:

☐ Have I talked to my child about why people want to save money?

☐ Does my child understand the phrase *pay yourself first?*

☐ Does my child understand that a bank or credit union is a safe place where we keep our money until we need it?

☐ Has my child opened a savings account at a bank or credit union?

☐ Have I talked with my child about putting a certain percentage aside for long-term savings?

☐ Have I thought about offering my child matching or interest on their income?

☐ Have I given my child opportunities to practice delaying gratification?

☐ Have I asked my child if there is anything she would like to save for?

☐ Have I helped my child create a personal financial goal?

☐ When my child achieves his weekly savings target, do I praise his accomplishment?

Chapter 5:

...

Earning

"Always do more than you get paid for as an investment in your future." Jim Rohn

There are two ways for kids to make money, actively and passively. Active income is money earned through trading your time for money. When kids mow the lawn, they are actively earning their income. Passive income is money earned through investments. If your child's mutual fund earned 6% interest in a year, the fund grew without your child having to do anything to make that happen. We want our kids to earn money through both paths. This chapter will explore active income and chapter 8 will explore passive income.

"Above-and-beyond" Jobs

Kids are going to spend a lot of their adult life working to earn money. So it's a good idea to give them hands-on experiences while they are still hanging out with you. With you they can learn about effort, time management, fair pay, and work ethic. And the bonus is that when kids have to work hard to earn money, it has more value to them and they tend to make better choices about what they do with it.

Depending on their age, the types of jobs kids can do come in many forms and are usually jobs that you would do but don't mind handing over to your kids for the purpose of having them earn extra money. For example, young kids can weed the garden while older kids mow the lawn. These are the above-and-beyond jobs. Remember, there are those *by default of being a family member* jobs where kids do not get paid (see Chapter 2).

Chew on This: Above-and-Beyond Jobs

Tell your kids that the allowance they receive may not be enough to get all the things they want. So you're willing to offer them a list of above-and-beyond jobs that they can do to earn extra money. With the help of your kids, come up with different types of jobs that your kids can do. Go over the expectations for each of the jobs and come up with reasonable fees. Keep in mind that some jobs will appeal to some kids and not to others. That's okay. Let your child choose from the list and do those he's interested in.

Possible above-and-beyond jobs:

- Shred paper

- Yard work (mow, weed, trim, rake, etc.)

- House work (windows, baseboards, blinds, etc.)

- Clean garage

- Wash/detail car

- Shovel snow

- Give the dog a bath

- Be creative…there's a lot of work to be done out there!

Above-and-Beyond Jobs

Job Description	Payment Amount

Starting Their Own Business/Working Outside the Home

It has been a pleasure to have Dani taking care of our pets for the past several months. We have really come to rely on her help and always look forward to her weekly visits. Her love for animals is apparent in how much she enjoys playing with the dogs when she arrives. We even admire how enthusiastically she does her work, even when she's cleaning out the bird and guinea pig cages! We would recommend Dani to any family looking for someone to take care of their pets.

What a powerful letter of recommendation. All because Dani was looking for ways to earn additional money and decided to tap into her interests.

Chew on This: Entrepreneurial Kids

There are several ways that kids can earn money working when they become adults. They can work for someone else as an employee. They can work for themselves and be self-employed. Or they can start their own business and have people work for them. This last group is made up of entrepreneurs.

Have your kids share one of their favorite stores or restaurants. Ask them if they know how their favorite place got started. They probably won't know but it probably started with an idea. People who come up with an idea and then turn it in to a profitable business are called entrepreneurs. Most likely their favorite store or restaurant started this way.

Then tell them that they could become entrepreneurs too. This way they have additional ways to earn extra money besides the above-and-beyond jobs. Lots of kids have started successful businesses. All they needed was an idea, a plan, support from their parents, and persistence. Lots of persistence. And before they knew it, they were making lots of money. From selling hair products and pencil toppers. Pencil toppers? Yup. Here's how.

Leanna Archer, at 13 years old, mixed her grandmother's secret formula for shampoo and handed it out to all her friends. They loved it and wanted more. Pretty soon word got out about this amazing shampoo and Leanna had to start making it in batches. Next thing you know, she was bringing in over $100,000 a year. And that was just the beginning. Her company and her product line keeps growing.

Then there's Jason O'Neill. What an amazing kid. He created little pencil toppers out of pipe cleaners and pompoms for a craft faire. People loved them so he made more. Just like Leanna, the next thing he knew, he was getting orders from all over the world. He won the Young Entrepreneur of the Year Award in 2007. He was eleven years old. Let me say that again. He was eleven years old. But here's the really cool thing. His first ventures started with the traditional lemonade stands and recycling. He got the "entrepreneurial bug" (literally....you should see his pencil toppers!) and, well, the rest, as they say, is history. Very cool.

It starts with discussing goods and services. Goods are products that we sell. Services are work that we do for someone else. Here is a starter list of goods and services that your kids may be interested in:

Goods	Services
• Candles	• Yard work
• Greeting cards	• House work
• Jewelry	• Pet sitting
• Birdhouses	• Car wash
• Baked goods	• Snow shoveling
• Pencil toppers!	• Christmas tree pick-up
(With parental help, kids can sell their wares on www.etsy.com)	• Grocery shopping
	• Garbage tote to curb
	• Babysitting
	• Website creation/computer stuff
	• Delivering papers
	• Tutoring
	• Soccer referee/baseball umpire

Have your kids think about their special talents, skills, and interests as a way to earn extra money and record them on the worksheet *My Special Talents, Skills, and Interests.* Skills can include being good at soccer or designing candles. But it can also include being responsible and reliable. Then have them think about ways they could use those skills to earn some extra money.

A great website, not only for ideas, but a great place to sell homemade items, is www.etsy.com.

If your child does express interest and has the time (school always comes first) there are a myriad ways for him to make extra money. As much as you can, offer support. Help him create fliers, drive him to his babysitting job, and lend him your rake. Your involvement lets him know that you take him seriously. And often, that's really all kids need to begin a budding business. Hey, it worked for Leanna and Jason.

Their First "Real" Job

Usually in the high school years, teens are interested in a part-time job beyond the home. It often corresponds with their access to the car keys. And as long as it doesn't interfere with their school work, it is a great thing to encourage. Not only does it provide them with useful life skills such as understanding the working world, but they earn a little extra gas money, as well.

This is typically the time an allowance is no longer provided. Teens learn to "support" themselves which often gives them a nice feeling of independence and helps build the confidence they will need when they do enter the "real world".

Some teens work only during the summer months then go back on their allowance during the school year. This still exposes them to the working world without interfering with their studies.

My Special Talents, Skills, and Interests

These are my special talents, skills, and interests:

List 3 ways that you could use your talents, skills, and interests to earn money:

How much would you charge? What supplies would you need? What would your costs be? Could you borrow items? How much profit could you make?

What steps would you need to take to set up your business? How would you get the word out about your new business?

Sample Flier

Christmas Tree

Pick-Up

Minimum Donation

$10.00

I am earning money to help pay for my trip to Squid Island, a sixth grade marine biology trip.

I would love to pick up your Christmas tree.

Pick-up Dates:

Dec. 28, 29, 30, 31 or Jan. 2, 3, 8, 9

Please call Ryan at: 555.1212

Leave your name, address, phone number, and pick-up day.

Thank you for your support!

Happy Holidays

My Money Reflections – Earning

Think about the activities in this chapter and answer the following questions:

☐ Do I have a list posted of "above-and-beyond" jobs my child can do to earn extra money?

☐ Have I discussed the expectations for the "above-and-beyond" jobs and the payment amount associated with each?

☐ Have I helped my child explore additional ways to earn extra money using his special talents, skills or interests?

☐ Does my child understand the difference between being an employee, self-employed, or a business owner/entrepreneur?

☐ Have I been as supportive as I can in helping my child pursue additional ways to earn extra money?

☐ Is my tween/teen interested in a part-time job? If so, have we discussed that it's okay to have an outside job just as long as school work comes first?

Chapter 6:

. . .

Spending

"The best things in life aren't things." Art Buchwald

"I spend it. What else am I supposed to do with it?"

This was the answer given by a fourth grader to the question, "What do you do with money when you receive it?" Good thing he was taking my money management class!

Unfortunately, that's the answer given by a lot of kids. Therefore, it's our job as parents and educators to teach our kids that spending is only one of several things we can do with our money. We actually have choices. Saving some of it is always a good idea. Sharing is another good idea. And then putting it to work for us, investing it, so that we can get even more money to save and share, is a great idea.

The biggest responsibility we have with money is learning how to manage it effectively so that we can have the things we need and want now while also saving for the future. Kids learn to save for the future by setting short- and long-term goals. First it's an ipod, then it's a car, then it's a down payment on a house. Somewhere in all of that is saving for retirement. The key is to teach them to spend less than they make. And it begins with understanding the difference between needs and wants.

Needs vs. Wants

Ask any kid if a Nintendo Wii is a need or a want and they will jokingly tell you that it's a need. Then they'll admit that, no, it's really a want.

Kids inherently know the difference between needs and wants. But they'll always try to get you to believe that their latest desire is a need. It's usually because you haven't had *The Talk* yet. You see, once you've had *The Talk*, it's harder for kids to get away with their little shenanigans. So have the talk. It goes something like this:

"How fortunate we are to be able to have all the things we need. What if we opened the pantry and there was nothing in it? Yikes. Or if we all only had one outfit to wear. That'd get pretty smelly after a while. I'm very happy that I'm able to provide you with food and clothing. And a nice, warm bed for you to sleep in. Those are definitely needs.

But it's also nice to have a few luxuries like that beautiful dress you just got or being able to go out to dinner like we did last night. Can you think of some other luxuries we have that we are thankful for?" (This puts them on the spot to acknowledge they know the difference between needs and luxuries/wants.)

This conversation makes it so much easier when you need to do something like, *"Hmmm. I know you need a new pair of shoes for school. But I'm not so sure the Nike Air Jordans fall into the need category. Can you find a pair that is in our budget? Or, if you like, you can pay the difference between what I'm willing to pay and the cost of these shoes."*

Knowing the difference between needs and wants helps kids prioritize their spending. Now, granted, most of the things they will be buying will probably fall in the 'wants' category. But even then, there are choices. *I want this new video game but if I spend my money on that then I won't be able to go bowling tomorrow with my friends. I think I'll pass on the video game.* This is called 'opportunity cost'.

Opportunity Cost

Simply put, opportunity cost is giving up the next best option as the result of getting something else. For example, your child has $10 to spend in the museum gift shop. There are two items she's interested in and both cost $8. She will need to choose one over the other. The one she gave up is the opportunity cost of getting to have the other one.

But there is another side to opportunity cost. Let's say your child found one item in the gift store she was interested in buying. She can choose to buy it and use up most of her $10. Or she can choose not to spend it. If she doesn't spend it, she can put it towards something else later, or save it and have it grow into even more money over time.

Here's a great illustration:

Buy the stuffed animal now:	Save the money and earn interest on it:
 Cost: $8.00 Money left: $2	$10.00 saved at 10% monthly interest (given by mom and dad!) $10.00 <u>+ 1.00</u>(interest the first month) $11.00 <u>+ 1.10</u>(interest the second month) $12.10

 Chew on This: Needs and Wants

Discuss needs and wants. A need is something you depend on. A want is something you would like but don't need.

- What is the difference between needs and wants? Give me an example of a need...a want.

- Is 'love' a need? How about 'friendship'?

- If you could have everything you wanted, how would that make you feel? Describe your day having everything you wanted.

- When you can't buy something you want, how does that make you feel? How do you get over this feeling?

- Do some people take care of their wants first before their needs? Why do you think they do this? What could this lead to?

- How do you think kids feel when they really want something but they or their parents don't have the money to get it?

- Why is it easier to spend someone else's money?

Activity: A fun exercise to do with younger kids to underscore needs vs. wants is to go through magazines and cut out pictures that represent needs and wants. Kids can glue these onto a piece of construction paper with the labels 'Needs' and 'Wants' at the top. You may find that this simple little activity lends itself to a lot of great discussion.

(By the way, explain that the pictures they cut out need to be of things we buy, not things like pictures of cute little babies. We don't buy those. So just make the rules clear. Because it happens. A lot. With girls.)

It Costs How Much?

Activity: Here's another fun thing to do with your tweens and teens. Have them take the *My Money Quiz* to see what they know about how much "stuff" costs. It will give your kids a greater appreciation for what everything really costs. Feel free to add your own items!

If you have more than one child taking the quiz, you can turn it into a fun game where the one who gets the closest to the right amount gets a point. For each point they get a Hershey's kiss...or whatever.

The *My Money Quiz* worksheet also asks kids to write down *about* how much money they have. It's always a good idea for kids to have a general idea of how much money they have. Just like adults, knowing this will help them make better decisions.

My Money Quiz Answers*	
Item	Cost**
Basketball shoes (Kohl's dept store)	$30.00
Pair of jeans (Kohl's dept store)	$30.00
Dinner out (Chili's) (sodas for everyone)	$45.00
iphone (8GB)	$99.00
iphone monthly service	$69.00/month
2-day pass to Disneyland	$141.00/person
4-door sedan (Honda Civic)	$18,500
College at 4-year state university (California)	$77,000
*Feel free to change some of these answers based on your shopping habits. **These "answers" reflect 2009 prices.	

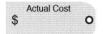

My Money Quiz

Where do you keep your money?

Write down *about how much* money you have. If you don't know, write *not sure*…then FIND OUT.

Now let's see what you know about how much stuff costs.

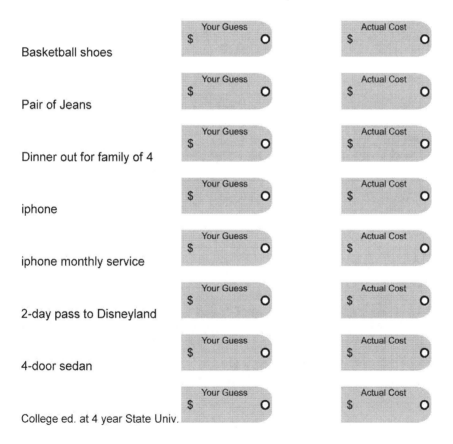

	Your Guess	Actual Cost
Basketball shoes	$	$
Pair of Jeans	$	$
Dinner out for family of 4	$	$
iphone	$	$
iphone monthly service	$	$
2-day pass to Disneyland	$	$
4-door sedan	$	$
College ed. at 4 year State Univ.	$	$

Being a Good Consumer

A consumer is someone who purchases goods and services. Being a good consumer is being careful about how you spend your money. In other words, a good consumer spends money wisely.

 Chew on This: How to be a Good Consumer

Discuss what it takes to be a good consumer by seeing how many ways your kids can come up with to spend money wisely. Some examples may include:

- researching before buying

- making a list

- using coupons

- comparison shopping

- waiting for sales

- finding out who has what you want and asking about their experiences with it

- buying when you know it's a good value

These all teach your child that you want to get the best value for your dollar. And getting the best value for your dollar does not necessarily mean that you have to get the cheapest item out there. There are times when spending a little extra for good quality will save you money in the long run.

Then tell your kids that another great way to spend money wisely is to ask yourself *Three Money Questions* before you spend even a penny:

- Do I need it?

- Can I afford it?

- Does it add value to my life?

Do I need it? This gives kids practice in thinking about the difference between needs and wants. If the item is clearly not a need, and for kids this is the majority of their spending, then at least they have acknowledged that they are pursuing and willing to plunk money down for a want. Which leads us to...

Can I afford it? This one is simple - if they don't have the money, they can't afford it. This is a good opportunity to help your child create a goal and work towards it.

Does it add value to my life? This takes time to learn. And you may need to spend some time discussing what 'value' means. Most kids will insist that they can't live without the particular item/experience and will move forward with their purchase. Revisit their decision after several days or weeks by having them reflect on whether or not their choice truly enriched their life. In other words, was it worth spending the money on? And give them time. Through experience, they will come to understand the true meaning of 'value'.

The key to the *Three Money Questions* is to model them with your kids. When considering a purchase, talk through the questions out loud so that your kids can "see" how decision-making happens.

Embracing Mistakes

> *"The man who makes no mistakes does not usually make anything."* John Edward Phelps

Allowing your kids to make money mistakes while they're still under your tutelage is important. Better now when the mistakes are cheaper. Although you may find it hard to let your child spend money on something you just know is a poor choice, it's important to let them experience the consequence. Consider it controlled failure. The key is to have the money conversation afterward. *Why did you make that choice? Was it a good one? How could you do it differently in the future?* Kids don't necessarily know how to work through problems unless we teach them. And teaching them how to effectively manage money by using the power of mistakes is a priceless opportunity!

Life is a Series of Choices

Piggy-backing on the previous section about making mistakes, learning how to make good choices is a very important life skill, not only in money but in other areas of our lives, as well. Since our choices can follow us for the rest of our lives, we need to teach kids how to make good ones. A good way to start is to ask them the reasoning behind their choices. *Why do you want to spend an extra $100 for that cell phone?* This gives them pause to make sure they are choosing for the right reasons.

Another technique to use that encourages the positive choices your child has made is to acknowledge them. *"I notice you've been hanging out a lot with Olivia. What is it that you like about her as a friend?"* Depending on her age, she may not have the exact words to describe her feelings so you may need to offer some suggestions. *"Is she a good listener? Does she respect your ideas?"* etc. Not only does this helps underscore that she has choices, but, again, you're teaching her how to think through her choices.

And teaching kids how to think through their choices before making a decision can help when those choices become even bigger: *Should I overextend on my house payments so that I can have a huge yard?* or *What kind of person do I choose to spend the rest of my life with?* The answers they come up with can greatly influence the quality of life they end up living.

Media Literacy

Media literacy is the ability to critique and analyze messages being sent to us through the media. And, boy, are we sent messages. Our kids are bombarded daily to spend money, look a certain way, and own certain things. Advertising **aimed at our kids** is a 15 billion dollar a year industry. It's next to impossible to remove them from this exposure – ads are everywhere…on t-shirts, billboards, shopping bags, television, radio, buses… They're even embedded into the TV shows we watch.

So we need to address the issue with our kids and teach them to think critically about the messages being sent. Advertising agencies are very good at getting us to think we need something when, in fact, we may not. They use celebrities and authority figures to help influence our spending decisions. And they're very good at appealing to our desires to fit in, have fun, and be hip. But as a parent, you want your kids to grow up with your values, not those of a marketing agency. And, like a lot of things in this book, it begins with a conversation.

Chew on This: Advertising

Ask your kids if they know what the Golden Arches are. Or what KFC stands for. Or any other symbol that you know your kids are familiar with. You can even hum them a jingle. Tell them that these symbols and tunes are the way a company brands its product. In other words, it's the way they get parents and kids to quickly recognize them and, hopefully, buy their product or service.

Then use the following questions to get them to think about the messages they are being sent.

- What are some other brand names that you know?

- Where do you see ads?

- Who pays for the ads?

- Describe some of your favorite ads or commercials. Why do they appeal to you? Does it make you want to buy the product or service?

- Why do companies advertise?

- Is advertising a bad thing?

- What kind of techniques do companies use to get you to buy their product? (bright colors, a jingle, logos, etc.)

- What message is the ad trying to get across? (it's the cool thing, a celebrity has it, wealthy people have it, it will make me happy, etc.)

- What affect does advertising have on our needs and wants?

- Do advertising messages encourage you to save more or spend more?

- Are there more facts or opinions in (this) ad?

- Is it okay for you not to have everything you see? Why?

- Does advertising influence your spending? If so, how?

- What things are popular at school? Do you feel you need to have it in order to fit in?

- What helps you decide to buy something?

- Have you ever bought something just because someone else had it?

- Have you ever bought something because of an ad and then been disappointed in it after you spent the money?

- When you have a financial goal, is it easier to turn down something you may have bought if you didn't have a goal?

- Did you know that if you feel bad about not having something, the ad has worked?

As you can see, this is a big topic and best done over several dinner chats. As you talk, be sure your kids know that spending money on products or services is not a bad thing; it keeps our economy going. But it's important to have a clear understanding of the marketing techniques used so that we are buying the products, they are not buying us.

Activity: Media Literacy

Hopefully you'll be able to resist TiVo'ing through some commercials in order to give your kids hands-on experiences with the world of advertising. Asking simple questions while you're watching TV will help teach your kids how to analyze the messages that are being sent. And the best part is that you'll really be teaching your kids how to think critically, and that's an important life skill.

Conversation questions to ask:

- Tell me when the commercial starts and when it ends. (This is to get young kids to focus on the difference between the watched program and commercials.)

- What is the commercial trying to sell?

- Is the commercial using facts or opinions?

- Who do you think paid for the commercial?

- Why do companies make commercials?

- What are they trying to get you to do?

- How are they trying to get you to buy their product?

- What values is the commercial emphasizing?

- Do you believe everything the commercial is saying? Explain.

It's YOU

But the absolute best way to teach kids how to spend money wisely is to model it yourself. Your kids are watching everything you do. Not on purpose. They just do it because it's how they learn to navigate in this world. So if you are always complaining about money, chances are your kids will grow up and do the same. If you recklessly spend money, your kids will probably, as well.

That doesn't mean you have to be perfect. But making an attempt to change your complaining and spending ways is a start. Involve your kids in your decision. Let them know that you're going to be trying really hard to make some changes and tell them what they are. Invite them to remind you as you drool over that got-to-have sweater. And having your kids see you make progress is probably one of the best ways to teach being persistent. You'll be giving them another important life skill.

Teachable Moment – Saying 'No' to Your Wants

Let's say you're out shopping with your kids. You see something you'd really like to have but you already know in your head you're not going to get it. This is the perfect time to teach your kids how you problem solved the steps you took to arrive at your decision. To underscore the lesson, you may need to ham it up a bit. It may seem silly at first but if you really want to teach your kids how to solve problems, they're going to need to "see" you solve some!

"Oh my gosh, this is soooooo cute! This would go perfect with my jeans. Yikes, it's a bit on the pricey side. And I don't really *need* a new shirt. Aaaaah…I've been trying hard not to put anything unnecessary on the credit card. If I was honest with myself, I already know it's more of a want. What to do? What to do? Well, I already know what the right thing to do is. I'm going to pass. (deep sigh). Okay, that wasn't so hard."

You get the idea. It will need to fit your style, but thinking out loud is such a powerful way to teach kids how to make decisions. There are times when direct teaching is the way to go. And there are other times, like this, when indirect teaching works best. It's the stealthy way to teach. And it can be a lot of fun!

Keeping Track

Now that your kids have a handle on needs and wants and ways to spend money wisely, it's time for your tweens and teens to keep track of their income and expenses. It is through keeping track that they will begin to see patterns in their spending over time. This is important because this will allow them the opportunity to make changes in their spending habits, if necessary.

Having your child keep his receipts from his purchases will help with this activity. In addition, keeping receipts in a file or envelope is good record-keeping practice and will come in handy if he ever finds himself needing to return an item.

Use the *Registry* worksheet to teach them how to record their income and expenses and keep a running balance. If you did the *Daily Income and Expenses Tracking Worksheet*, from Chapter 2, they're already familiar with keeping track.

While your kids keep track they'll be learning new vocabulary such as income, expense, and balance. As you use this new vocabulary, your kids will become more comfortable with it. Knowing and understanding the language of money is an important step towards financial literacy.

Activity: Registry Reflections

After **at least** two weeks of recording in the Registry (four is best) review the list. Have your child rate all the items from 1 - 10, 10 being your child would buy it again. Discuss the results. This is a great way to get kids to reflect on their spending choices and a good way for you to teach them strategies for making better choices in the future. Some strategies may include:

- asking the three money questions before making a purchase

- waiting at least two days before buying the item

- reflect on the opportunity cost (if I hadn't spent the money I could have put it towards...)

- asking yourself why you thought you needed the item

Registry

Date	Description	Expenses	Income	Balance
	Beginning balance			

Checking Accounts/Debit Cards

At some point it will become important to teach your child how to use a checking account. Once she has proved to you that she can manage money well – that's the time. If you've done all of the activities so far in this book, it tends to be around age 15 or 16. And the best part of the checking account is that it comes with a debit card. At least, it should. Some banks and credit unions are reluctant to give teenagers debit cards. And for good reason. But if you are confident that your child is ready, they will usually make an exception as long as you give your written permission. Sometimes they ask to see student grades, as well.

Teens love getting checking accounts with debit cards. It makes them feel grown up. Remind them that responsible grownups keep track of their spending in their registry. If they've followed the steps in this guide, they'll have experience recording income and expenses in a registry.

Keeping track is important because debit cards are connected to your child's checking account. Every time your child swipes her card, the money gets pulled from her account. So she's going to need to be very careful. Banks are notorious for finding ways to get a few extra dollars from you in the form of overdraft fees. And it's nothing to sneeze at. The average overdraft fee is $28. For a teen, that's a lot of gas money. As of this writing, laws are being drafted so that bank customers will need to opt *in* to an overdraft protection plan. Make sure you are familiar with the terms of the account.

 Activity: Writing Checks

With their checking account, your child will also receive checks. It's not that often that we write checks any more but it happens just often enough that we need to teach our kids how to do it. A fun way to do this is simply to have your tween or teen write your next check out for you. Since most people have moved to online bill paying, you'll need to be watching out for the next time you pull out your checkbook. Then, instead of filling out all the information yourself, teach your child how to do it. Kids love acting grown up and since the check is real and will actually be mailed…it is grown up! Show him how to keep track of it in your registry. And although the signature on the check will need to be yours, have him practice writing his own signature (they LOVE this!) for the time when the check he fills in will actually be his.

Chew on This: Those Plastic Cards

Ask your kids what they know about credit cards, debit cards, and ATM cards. Even five- and six-year olds have an "idea" about what they are. Their answers may surprise you. And it may lead you to be thankful you're having this dinner discussion!

Then make sure they have accurate information:

Debit/ATM Card: Tied in with a checking and/or account and draws money directly from the account. Sometimes the debit or ATM card has the Visa or Mastercard logo on it. That just allows the card to be used at all the locations a regular Visa or Mastercard can be used. The money is still drawn directly from the account.

It's important to keep a running record of all purchases. Watch for overdraft fees with debit/ATM cards. The bank is "nice" enough to cover overdrafts, but they will charge upwards of $28 for each overdraft you incur. The good news is, as of this writing, laws are being drafted where bank customers will need to opt-in on the overdraft protection plans.

Credit Cards: Credit cards, on the other hand, allow the user to borrow money. That's right. It's a loan. Although we will discuss credit cards in further detail in Chapter 9, right now your kids need to know that if they don't pay off their credit cards each month, they will have to pay even more money in the form of interest. Credit card use requires responsibility and discipline. Let me say that again. Credit card use requires responsibility and discipline.

Those Other Debit Cards

Debit cards are becoming more and more available. The banks and organizations that distribute them want you to be convinced that we live in a plastic world and, therefore, offering these cards to our kids is really helping our kids and us out. But the fees alone for having the "privilege" of using these cards can be quite hefty. See the chart on the next page.

If, and only IF, your child has had plenty of hands-on experiences with money, understands the value of money, knows the difference between needs and wants, has made and learned from their money mistakes, knows how to set a personal financial goal and then has achieved it, then, and ONLY then, do I recommend use of these other cards.

Why? Because unless your child has experienced all of the money skills listed in the previous paragraph, there will be a disconnect between real money and plastic money. And research shows that people spend more when they use plastic. Not what we want our kids to be doing. Here's an example your kids will be able to relate to:

People who use plastic to pay for their fast food will spend an average of 51% MORE than those who use cash. Plastic is convenient. That's why a lot of people like it. But it's too convenient if you don't have the skills to be responsible and disciplined.

Some of those other debit cards being pushed on tweens and teens:

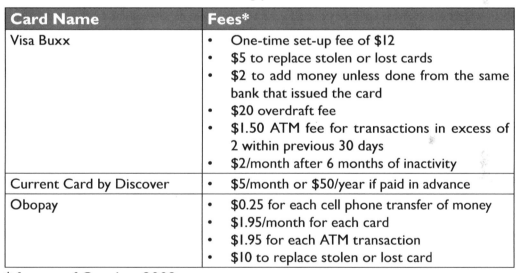

Card Name	Fees*
Visa Buxx	• One-time set-up fee of $12 • $5 to replace stolen or lost cards • $2 to add money unless done from the same bank that issued the card • $20 overdraft fee • $1.50 ATM fee for transactions in excess of 2 within previous 30 days • $2/month after 6 months of inactivity
Current Card by Discover	• $5/month or $50/year if paid in advance
Obopay	• $0.25 for each cell phone transfer of money • $1.95/month for each card • $1.95 for each ATM transaction • $10 to replace stolen or lost card

* fees as of October 2009

My Money Reflections – Spending

Think about the activities in this chapter and answer the following questions:

☐ Does my child understand that with money comes choices?

☐ Have I discussed the difference between needs and wants with my child?

☐ Does my child understand that there are levels to needs and wants?

☐ Does my child know about how much money she has?

☐ Does my child have a better appreciation for the price of different things?

☐ Have I explained the idea of opportunity cost?

☐ Have I discussed with my child different ways to be a good consumer?

☐ Does my child know how to use the *Three Money Questions*?

☐ Have I allowed my child to make spending mistakes? If so, have I helped him come up with strategies on how to do it differently next time?

☐ Have I helped my child reflect on the reasons behind the choices she wants to make?

☐ Does my child know that companies are in business to make money and one way to try and get us to buy their products or services is through advertisements?

☐ Have I helped my child analyze an ad or commercial?

☐ Am I a good spending role model for my child? If not, what am I doing to change that?

☐ Has my child had practice recording his income and expenses while keeping a running balance?

☐ Have I looked for opportunities to help my child make better spending choices?

☐ Is my teen ready for a checking account? If so, have I helped her open one?

☐ Have I taught my teen/tween how to fill out a check?

☐ Does my teen understand how a debit card works?

Chapter 7:

· · ·

Budgeting

If you don't manage money,
it will manage you.

The word 'budget' often gets a bad rap. People equate it with work. And a sense of not being allowed to enjoy money. It doesn't need to be that way. In fact, we should start right now to use the word over and over again with our kids without cringing. Budget, budget, budget, budget, yippee, budget, budget.

Why? Because it's through taking a close look at how much money we're bringing in and where we're choosing to spend it that we can begin to build our wealth. And building wealth is a good thing - so we need to budget. Besides, once we've done it, it's okay not to do it again for awhile.

Believe it or not, it's actually easy to do with kids. And since you're going to be skipping around the room every time you use the word, your kids will be anxious to get started.

By default, young kids already budget. That's because they really don't have many expenses. In fact, they don't have any at all. They get money then they decide what to spend it on. And most often they only spend what they have.

As our kids get a little older, they begin to add on responsibilities. Maybe they have to pay for school lunches now. Or part of their cell phone bill. It's when they begin to have regular expenses that a budget comes in to play. But you can still create a budget with your child regardless. Here's how.

Activity: Budgeting

You're going to need the *Registry* worksheet from the previous chapter. If you haven't done so already, help them figure out what their current balance is by adding up all the money they have. Record this in the registry. As they receive income or spend money, show them how to record it to keep a runing balance.

When you have **one month's** worth of data, gather some colored pencils. Color-code all the same type of items in the registry. For example, if your child spends money on snack-type foods, then highlight all those items with the same color. Add up the amounts in that 'snack' category. That's about how much your child can expect to spend each month in that category, although at this age, this amount can vary greatly. Round this total so that you have an easier number to work with. In the example on the next page, the 'snack' category added up to $9.82. It was rounded to $10. Do that with all the color-coded categories, including income, then transfer the data to the *My Budget* worksheet.

Registry - Sample

Date	Description	Expenses	Income	Balance
			Beginning balance	$53.49
9/5/09	Bubble gum	1.12		52.37
9/7/09	Paper Route		45.00	97.37
9/10/09	Fundraiser - cookies	4.50		92.87
9/12/09	Library fine	1.00		91.87
9/12/09	Used DVD	15.00		76.87
9/15/09	Mini golf	6.00		70.87
9/15/09	In n Out burgers	2.31		68.56
9/16/09	Yard work		15.00	83.56
9/22/09	Movies	15.00		68.56
9/25/09	Slurpee	1.89		66.67
9/25/09	Bowling	9.00		57.67
9/30/09	Allowance		20.00	77.67
9/30/09	Charity	8.00		69.67
9/30/09	Long-term savings	8.00		61.67

My Budget - sample

Monthly Income Categories	
Paper route	$ 45.00
Allowance	$ 20.00
Extra Chores	$ 15.00
	$
Total Monthly Income	$ 80.00
Monthly Expense Categories (include savings and charity)	
Long-term savings - 10%	$ 8.00
Entertainment	$ 30.00
Snacks	$ 10.00
Charity - 10%	$ 8.00
Electronics (DVDs, video games, itunes)	$ 15.00
Other	$ 1.00
Total Monthly Expenses	$ 72.00

Total Monthly Income	$ 80.00
(Subtract) Total Monthly Expenses	$ 72.00
Monthly left-over	$ 8.00

Category	Monthly Expense	Total Yearly Expense
snacks	$ 10.00 x 12	$ 120.00

Next budget review scheduled for: _____

To underscore how little amounts can add up, choose one of the expense categories and multiply the amount by 12 months. It's usually an eye-opening experience to see how much just two trips a week to a burger joint can cost over the course of a year! This is a good example of opportunity cost, giving up one thing to have another thing.

Now help them analyze their budget. How much are they spending in each category? Are there areas where money can be saved? Is it possible to set up some personal financial goals with the money left over?

That last question is an important one. That's where the wealth-building comes in. Although we'll cover this in greater detail in the next chapter, it's important to note that even small amounts of money over time can grow into lots of money. So one less slurpee at the mall *can* make a difference. Remember, it's about choices. Creating a budget helps us find those choices.

Notice how the balance in our sample account has over $55. Just because we have the money doesn't mean we have to spend it. Pretty soon it's going to be time for this child to take that money and put it to work for her. That's when she'll learn all about investing which is covered in Chapter 8.

When we teach kids at an early age how to live within the confines of the tangible money they have, they learn it is possible. And they can do it while still enjoying that treat every now and again. After all, what's the point of earning money if we can't enjoy it, too?

How Often?

This is the nice thing about having kids create a budget. Once they do it, they don't really need to do it again for a while. People often assume it's a monthly chore but it doesn't have to be that way. Once you see that your goals are being met, for example, that you are automatically saving 10% of your income, you're good to go.

That said, it is important to do a periodic review, maybe every six months or so. Just to make sure to stay on track. So go ahead and put it on the calendar. Now.

My Budget

Monthly Income Categories	
	$
	$
	$
Total Monthly Income	
Monthly Expense Categories (include savings and charity)	
	$
	$
	$
	$
	$
	$
	$
Total Monthly Expenses	$

Total Monthly Income	$
(Subtract) Total Monthly Expenses	$
Monthly left-over	$

Category	Monthly Expense	Total Yearly Expense
	$ x 12	$

Next budget review scheduled for: _____

Teachable Moments- Spending Within the Limits of a Specific Budget

Back-to-School Shopping: Tweens and teens are quite capable of shopping for themselves. They may make some mistakes along the way, but they're learning. So giving them a lump sum of money and putting them in charge of spending within the limits of the budget is good practice.

A great time to do this is when it's time to go back-to-school shopping. Since you're going to be spending money anyway, why not use it as an opportunity to give your kids hands-on experiences with budgeting?

Begin by making a list of needed items. You can decide to lump everything together or create separate lists such as one for clothes and one for office-type supplies. Then decide how much you are willing to spend in each category.

Get CASH in the needed amount. This helps underscore the value of a dollar (it makes a difference if you can SEE the money) and helps them stick to the budget. When your child runs out of money, he's done. This helps underscore that lesson of living within our means. But your child will probably be using all those great tips you taught him about being a good consumer (see chapter 6), so you don't have to worry about him running out. As an added incentive for him to get the best deals, tell him that any money left over is his to keep. Just make sure he buys all the stuff he needs!

Birthday Party: Another hands-on activity that tweens and teens can do to experience the idea of budgeting is to have them plan, and then shop for, their birthday party. This is also an awesome way to teach them the importance of being organized. They're going to need to consider the number of guests, party games, food, party favors, paper plates, etc. You could even take it to the next level and have them come up with the "flow" of the party...when to play games, when to eat, etc.

My Shopping List

My budget is $ _____

These are the things I need to buy:

This is how much I spent: $_____ This is how much I have left over $_____

Activity: The Family Budget

Supplies needed: play money in a variety of denominations

Talk to your kids about what a budget is. Very simply, a budget is a plan for your money. Discuss the reasons why it's important to know how much money you are bringing in and how much is going out. (So you can live within the means of your budget.)

Ask your kids if they can come up with different categories where your money is spent each month. Give them an example like rent/mortgage.

Typical Categories:

- Rent/mortgage
- Car payment/maintenance
- Utilities
- Phone
- Insurance (home and auto)
- Medical (includes health insurance)
- College fund
- Food
- Clothing
- Vacation
- Entertainment (includes going out to dinner, movies, concerts, etc.)
- Electronics

For tweens and teens, talk about the difference between fixed and variable expenses. A fixed expense is a known amount, like the mortgage. A variable expense can change from month to month, like utilities.

Hand everyone $100 in play money. Tell them that before they can enjoy the entertainment and electronics categories, they need to pay the monthly bills. Then go down the list and have them hand you the amount owed for each of the categories, which is listed below. You may need to help the younger ones make trade-ins of their bills so they have the correct denominations to pay with. This is a great math exercise.

Of course, feel free to change the categories and the amounts associated with each. For example, I did not include a category for the college fund and some parents feel strongly about that. I also didn't include a category for credit card payments. Tailor it to fit your family. In fact, with a little number crunching, you can make it a reduced version of the real thing!

Category	Cost/month
Rent/mortgage	$25
Long-term saving	$10
Medical	$5
Food	$15
Utilities (water, gas, electricity)	$10
Car/gas	$10
Phone/cable	$3
Clothes/haircuts, etc	$4
TOTAL	$82

Along the way your kids will probably complain about handing over so much money. This is a great opportunity to talk about how expensive it is just to do the everyday stuff. All 'needs' must get paid. We can't go without food, shelter, or clothing. Discuss some ways that it might be possible to reduce spending in these necessary categories. Examples may be to shop at bargain stores or choose a smaller house.

At this point, your child should have $18 left. They are now going to use that left-over money to choose from the categories in the table below. Sometimes kids are reluctant to spend any more of their money, so the rule is they have to choose at least two other categories. We don't want them to turn into little penny pinchers.

Category	Cost
Charity	Choose between $2-10
Vacation	
Out-of-state	$5
Close to home	$3
Eating out	$3
Entertainment (movies, concerts, bowling, etc)	$5
Toys, electronics, etc.	$5

Discuss their choices. Then discuss how much money they have left over. What do they plan on doing with the money? Ask them what they learned from this activity.

If you're comfortable with it, having your older kids actually help you pay the monthly bills can be an enlightening experience for them.

Chew on This: Saving Money in the Family Budget

Revisit the family budget but this time, choose an area that everyone can help reduce spending. Good ones for families to do together are utilities or entertainment. Then come up with an amount that you want to reduce that category by for the upcoming month. For example, you may want to reduce spending for utilities by $40.

Discuss ways everyone can chip in to help save money in that category. For utilities, some ideas may be: turn off lights when leave room; turn thermostat down/up 1-2 degrees, shorter showers, not keeping refrigerator door open long, check insulation, etc.

Then, and this is the fun part, decide what you're going to do with the savings. This also helps get everyone on board. Will it go towards a fun night out with the family or maybe towards tickets to a theme park? Although the idea is to save money and now you're deciding on ways to spend it, remember, you are also establishing healthy conservation habits which will continue long after you've had that fun night out.

Teachable Moment

The Cell Phone: Parents have been handed an unbelievable tool to help teach their tweens and teens money management. The cell phone. Yup. That object of love and hate. Done correctly it becomes an object of learning. Here's how.

Teens need to stay connected to their friends. This is normal as they figure out their place in the world. Cell phones keep them connected. Using their "need" for a cell phone as the motivator, we can teach them basic money management skills such as budgeting and paying bills.

First, tweens and teens need to know that along with a cell phone comes responsibility. Keeping track of your cell phone, resisting the temptation to text during dinner, and paying your phone bill. Kids paying bills? You bet! And the best time to teach them is while they're still hanging out with you.

Next, it's important to establish what part of the phone bill your child is responsible for. For example, you may pay the family plan fee but maybe your teen pays the additional phone line fee, texting, and any upgrades.

Now comes the fun part. Kids learn to manage their money in the context of something they love...their cell phone! Upgrades? They pay. Overages? They pay. New phone? They pay. Lost phone? They pay. Unpaid bill? No phone. See how simple it is? Okay, so it's going to take a few months before everyone understands how the whole thing works, but when that happens, it's a thing of beauty. Kids are happy; as long as they pay the bill, they stay connected to friends. Parents are happy; their kids are learning real life skills. It's a win/win.

Although a lot of parents are willing to pay for their kids' cell phones because it offers peace of mind, how about the peace of mind that comes with knowing your child is ready to take on the financial challenges that await her out there? Don't miss this silver-platter opportunity. With tweens and teens, when you get the chance, take it.

My Money Reflections - Budgeting

Think about the activities in this chapter and answer the following questions:

☐ Does my child understand what a budget is?

☐ Am I careful about not turning the word 'budget' into a negative word around my child?

☐ Have I shown my child how to record his income and expenses in the Registry?

☐ Does my child know how to keep a running balance?

☐ Have I helped my child review her Registry and color-code similar items?

☐ Have I helped my child multiply one of the spending categories out 12 months to see the total amount spent in one year?

☐ Have I helped my child determine if there are areas he can cut back on spending?

☐ Have I scheduled the next budget review with my child…and put it on the calendar?

☐ Have I given my child real-life opportunities to experience shopping within the limits of a budget?

☐ Does my child have a greater appreciation for all the different categories of the family budget that need to be paid each month?

☐ Have we gone over ways we can all contribute to reducing spending in certain categories of the family budget?

☐ Is my tween/teen ready for the responsibility of a cell phone? If so, what portion of the bill will she be paying for?

Chapter 8:

. . .

Investing

There is power to compound interest.
Those who understand that, col-
lect it. Those who don't, pay it.

Albert Einstein, a very intelligent man, called compound interest the eighth wonder of the world. And for good reason. Think about this: If you socked away $100 every month into an investment that averaged a 6% annual return beginning when you were 18 years old and kept it up until you retired at 65, you'd end up with $313,187.

And if you were getting an average yearly return of 10%, your money would sky rocket to $1,281,919.

Not bad. It's all about the compound interest.

Compound interest is money that grows on itself. Here's how it works: If you invest $100 at 10% monthly interest (no, I don't know of any place other than the bank of mom and dad that does this!), by the end of the month you'll have $110 ($100 + $10 interest). By the end of the next month you'll have $121 ($110 + $11 interest). That's because you earn interest on the interest already earned. Do this for several years and, well, it's a ridiculous amount of money.

Passive Income

The beauty of compound interest is that kids are earning money but they're doing it in a way that doesn't require them to actively do any work. It's all earned passively. Ever heard the phrase *building wealth*? Passive income, in this case in the form of compound interest, is a key to building wealth. The work is done once and the payout continues forever, as long as you have the investment. Instead of you working for your money, your money is working for you. (Some people describe the passive income received from stocks and bonds as *portfolio income*.)

Seeing is ~~Believing~~ Understanding

 Activity: Passive Income

To really underscore the power of compound interest, try these activities:

All ages: KidsSave, a kids' savings and money management software program (www.kidnexions.com). Download the trial version of the program. It's free. Set up an account for your child. Have your child log into their account and experiment around with customizing the monthly interest rate in the *What-If* section. The results are reflected visually in graph form.

Tweens/teens: The yarn activity: A quick, easy hands-on activity involves using two different colored pieces of yarn.

Materials Needed:
- Yarn in two different colors
- Scissors
- Ruler
- Tape
- Calculator

The story: A pair of twins decide they want to save their money. One chooses to hide $100 every month in his mattress. The other decides to put the $100 in a mutual fund. Over time, that mutual fund averaged 6% annual interest. How did each of the siblings do after 47 years of socking their money away?

1. Have your child cut one 31" length of yarn. As she is measuring, make sure not to pull the yarn too tight as when she "let's go" the yarn will "shrink".

2. Have her take the other colored yarn and cut a piece that is 5 ½ inches long.

3. Compare the two pieces of yarn. The 31" piece represents investing the money in the mutual fund. The 5 ½ piece is the mattress money.

4. Have your child tape the two ends together so that the comparison is easily made. Tell her that the 5 ½ piece represents $56,400. That is the amount you get when you save $100 each month from age 18 to 65. The 31" represents $313,187, the amount you get when earning 6% annual interest from age 18 to 65.

5. Now have her look at the difference between the two pieces. This represents the amount of interest that grew by keeping the money invested: $256,787.

6. Reinforce the idea that the $256,787 is free money. She didn't need to do anything to earn it except let it grow. It's passive income!

Try the same yarn activity, but this time the twins don't begin until they're 25 years old.

1. Cut a 20" inch length of yarn and a 5" length in a different color.

2. The 20" represents $199,149 collected by the twin who put the $100 in a mutual fund every month. The 5" represents $48,000 from the other twin who put the money in the mattress.

3. The difference between the two pieces: $151,149. That's the interest earned. It's free!

Discuss the moral of the story: The earlier you begin investing, the more money you'll make. Another way to say it is: The longer you keep your money invested, the larger it will grow.

The Keys to Compounding

The yarn activity reflects the three keys to compounding:

- Time (47 years – starting at age 18 and ending at 65)
- Amount invested ($100/mo)
- Growth rate (6% annually)

Time: Our kids have lots of it. It's up to us to help them take advantage of it.

Amount invested: We need to teach our kids to save some of the money they earn through allowance, above-and-beyond jobs, part-time jobs, and gift money so they can begin investing it. The good news is, kids can begin investing with as little as $10!

Growth rate: There are a lot of different investment options for our kids. They come on a continuum of low risk to high risk which is directly associated with the growth rate, the amount earned passively on a yearly basis.

$ Chew on This: Ask your tween or teen which they think is the better deal: starting with a beginning balance of $100 and either receiving $5 each week for allowance or getting 10% monthly interest? If you've done the yard activity with them, they should know the answer to this! (It's the interest!) If you set up this scenario in KidsSave, kids can quickly see the value of opting for interest.

I Don't Know Anything About Investing. How Can I Possibly Guide My Child?

Most parents are in this category so you are not alone. And you're very lucky. Not only will your kids be learning about investing, but they're going to be learning how to learn – through watching you learn. You and your child are going to hop on to www.fool.com and www.bankrate.com and figure out the best first investment for your child. Consider it parent/child bonding time. To help get you started, though, read the section *Investment Options* below. And to offer another tip, CDs and mutual funds are great first investments for kids.

Risk Tolerance

Whenever you invest money, you are taking on some risk. Taking on risk means that there is a possibility that you may not get what you want. In fact, you may even lose. Some investment vehicles are much less risky than others. In looking at the graphic on the next page, savings accounts, money markets, CDs and bonds are less risky than mutual funds or the stock market. That's because the amount of return for less risky investments can be significantly smaller than for the riskier ones. Since kids have a pretty long time horizon, investing in mutual funds and individual stocks, can pay off nicely in the long run.

Even so, when kids begin investing, it is a good idea for them to know that they should only invest what they can afford to lose. If they want to buy $100 of stock in ABC Company with the goal of making a decent profit, are they also willing to lose that $100 and end up with nothing? In fact, asking them this question and then watching their reaction is a good way to determine whether or not they're ready to begin investing.

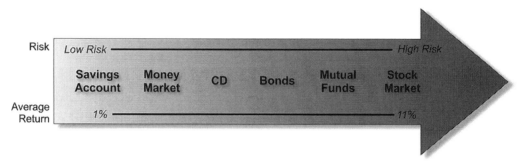

At What Age

When your child can understand that an investment is a long-term commitment, 4-5 years or longer, and he knows the basics of the different investment options (on the next page), and he's willing to lose the amount he invests, he's ready to begin investing. You may even want him to read and discuss with you the chapters in *The Motley Fool's Investment Guide for Teens* which offers a pretty good synopsis for beginning investors. Some kids are ready at age 10, others not until their teens.

Since your child is not of legal age, you'll need to set up custodial accounts for his investments. It's easy to do and simply includes your name on the investment. You'll set these up as you make the investments.

If you want to start your child off slowly and get a feel for his investing "personality", go virtual. Your kids can play a variety of investing games and create their own portfolios, without the worry of losing real money. http://virtualstockexchange.com/Game/Homepage.aspx

Investment Options

Investment Type	Description	Things to Know	Where do I find these?
Savings Account	A place to keep money that is easily accessible .	Deposit with FDIC insured banks or NCUA insured credit unions.	Bank/credit union
Money Market Fund	A place to keep money that is easily accessed. A mutual fund that buys short-term, low risk securities*.	Minimum deposit required. Earns a little more than a savings account. Not FDIC insured, but still pretty safe.	Bank/credit union
CDs (certificate of deposit)	Time-based, fixed rate of return investment.	CDs offer a higher rate than a savings or money market account and is a great first investment. Your child will need to relinquish the money for 3 months to 5 years. But, heck, all they have is time. FDIC insured.	Bank/some brokerages
Bonds	Loans to the local, state, or federal government, or even a corporation.	Bonds offer a higher rate than a savings or money market account and are out of reach until their maturity date, the date you can get your money. Backed by the US government (except corporate bonds)	Most financial institutions
Mutual Funds	A collection of stocks and bonds.	An investment made up of a pool of funds. Allows investors to have access to a diversified group of stocks and bonds. Not FDIC insured.	Brokerages
Stock	A certificate representing one unit of ownership in a company.	More of a long term investment. Not FDIC insured.	Brokerages , some companies will sell stock directly to you

*stocks and bonds

The ABCs of Mutual Funds

Mutual funds are made up of the stocks of a lot of different companies. Sometimes those companies share an industry, say technology. Or a goal such as being socially conscious. Then, through a broker, people, lots and lots of people, pool their money together to buy shares. Watch for fees, though. No-load funds are those that don't charge you to buy or sell your shares.

The ABCs of Individual Stocks

The internet makes buying and selling stocks pretty easy. Stocks are ownership in the company the stock came from. Kids love the idea that they own a piece of their favorite shoe or clothing store! You can buy stocks through broker-ages and there are myriad online brokerages for you to choose from. Just type 'brokerage' into your search engine and watch what comes up. Pick one that meets your needs and budget.

If you don't want to go through a broker and your child can make small investments (as small as $10 each) on a regular basis, you may want to consider DRIPs. These are dividend reinvestment plans and are offered directly through the company itself. The advantage here is something called dollar-cost averaging. That's when you buy in at different prices that tend to average out over time in an upwardly direction. Again, type 'drip' into your search engine.

Which companies should your kids invest in? A simple *what are you interested in* is a great place to start. Your child may choose companies that are familiar to them like McDonalds or Disney. They may choose companies where they love to shop or their favorite burrito restaurant. Maybe they want to invest in a company that is socially responsible. Let them guide you.

Then do a little research online with your child. Go to the company's website and find out: How long has the company been around? What kind of debt do they owe? What is their stock history like? What are their earnings? What are people saying about it?

Also, you'll want to search the internet for articles and additional information to help you make an informed decision.

Again, watch for fees.

A personal note: My youngest son wanted to invest in Chipotle, his favorite burrito joint. We made an appointment with our broker so he could get the experience in talking with an expert. During the meeting, the broker showed him how to use the brokerage firm's website to find out information on his chosen company and to see the firm's rating of the stock. When my son saw the grade of 'D' as the rating, he decided not to invest.

Several months passed and he kept watching the stock slowly rise. Then he read an article that recommended Chipotle as a 'buy'. He decided his time was right and made the purchase. Within six months the stock had doubled in price! He cashed out his equity and invested it in Costco, his favorite place to eat samples on the weekend.

The moral of the story: Do your own research. Had my son stuck with the brokerage firm's rating, he would have lost the opportunity.

Diversifying

Over time make sure that your child diversifies her investments. Take a look at the total amount of money your child has and allocate a percentage of that to different investments. You could start off with 5% in CDs and bonds, another 5% in mutual funds, and an additional 5% in carefully chosen companies. You don't want her to have all of her eggs in one basket and then watch all those eggs fall and break. Over time you'll adjust the percentages.

And always keep in mind that investing is for the patient. It generally takes years for compound interest to work its magic. That said, always keep an eye on your investments and teach your child to do the same. Checking in on them once a year is recommended.

My Money Reflections – Investing

Think about the activities in this chapter and answer the following questions:

☐ Have I illustrated the power of compound interest to my child?

☐ Does my child know that he is in a great position in terms of investing his money…that he has time (one of the keys to compounding) on his side?

☐ Have I explained the difference between active and passive income?

☐ Does my child know that there are other places besides a savings account to keep her money where it will grow faster over time?

☐ Have I spent some time online with my child researching different investment options?

☐ Have I discussed with my child his risk tolerance?

☐ Have I explained that if my child decides to invest in the stock market, she agrees that it is a long-term investment and she cannot get emotionally attached to her stocks?

☐ Does my child have any special interests that could help him decide which companies he wants to invest in?

☐ Have I explained to my child that, over time, she will need to diversify her investments?

Chapter 9:

. . .

Things Your Child Should Know

"If you think education is expensive, try ignorance." Derek Bok

Credit Cards

Credit card debt is the most expensive debt you can have.

Credit cards have become a way of life. We have a love/hate relationship with them. On the one hand, they're convenient and necessary to help build credit. On the other hand, one slip up could end up costing a lot of money. **Credit cards require responsibility and discipline.**

Kids should not be using credit cards. Period. They need to spend their time learning how to be responsible with real money. That said, it is still important to teach them about what credit cards are and how they are to be used…when they eventually get to use them.

First, they need to know that credit card use is a form of borrowing. And unless we pay our balance off each month, we incur interest charges, just like a loan. Would it ever occur to you to take out a loan for a new pair of shoes? It almost sounds ridiculous. But people do it all the time with nary a thought.

Remember back in the last chapter when kids experimented around with 6% compound interest? Wasn't it cool to see how much free money they could get just by putting small amounts of money aside each month? Now think of the opposite of that coolness. Where your debt can grow even faster. You saw what 6% could do over time. Consider what 21% can do over time!

Credit cards are an abstract idea. It's hard for young kids to get a hold of what they really are. After all, they simply see you swipe it when you want something. Here's what you need to start teaching them:

- When you use your card, you are borrowing money at a very high interest rate
- Using your credit card is also the same as taking out a loan
- It's important to pay off your card each month or you will have to pay extra money (finance charge)
- Finance charges can be upwards of 28%
- You will have the opportunity to get a card or two one day. You need one to help build your credit. You need to build your credit so that you can get good loans for big things like a car or a house
- You will also need good credit to do things like rent an apartment
- Only if you use your card wisely you will build good credit

For those of you who carry balances, set up a plan to pay off your card(s) and then include your child in watching the balance go down. This will show her that it takes hard work and discipline. But always underscore the message that the best way not to be in that position is to start off paying the balance each month. And that way, you'll be in a better position to take advantage of some of the rewards programs that different cards offer.

Gambling/Lottery

Which has a better chance of happening to you...winning the lottery or being struck by lightning?

You've probably figured out that it's being struck by lightning. Or getting into a car or plane crash. But 1/3 of the U.S. population thinks that winning the lottery is the only way to financial security. Yikes. Let's get our kids educated.

A typical lottery ticket asks you to choose 6 numbers from 1 – 50. You have a 1 in 15,800,000 chance of choosing the same numbers as the winning ticket.

You have a 1 in 280,000 chance of getting struck by lightning.

You'll get struck by lightning way before you win the lottery.

Here's another question: Which takes more of your money, the lottery or casino gambling?

You may be surprised to find that the lottery keeps more of your money. Casinos typically keep 5% of your money while the lottery keeps 50%. That's 10 times more! That doesn't mean that you can't have fun every now and then. But if it becomes a part of your routine, there's a problem.

By the way, 20% of the people buy 80% of the lottery tickets. They are usually low income people.

 Chew on This: Playing the Lotto

While you're enjoying chicken parmesan together, hand everyone a piece of paper and a pencil. Tell them you're going to gamble. They usually love to hear an adult say that. Then ask them to think of 6 random numbers from 1 – 50. Give an example such as *you can choose the day of your birthday or your favorite number or just randomly pick numbers.*

Then tell them that if they can match **any two** of your numbers regardless of order they'll get (think of something small that they would like such as a slurpee at the mall). Then tell them that if they match all of your numbers correctly you'll give them (think of some great big prize. Don't worry, the odds are they won't guess your numbers!)

Then everyone secretly writes their numbers. On your piece of paper write six consecutive numbers such as 1, 2, 3, 4, 5, 6 or 50, 49, 48, 47, 46, 45. Chances are they won't be writing consecutive numbers.

When everyone is ready, share out. There's usually a lot of discussion at this point. Sometimes someone matches a number and they're a winner! Slurpee time. But mostly, no one wins. Discuss the odds and whether or not spending money on lottery tickets is a good idea.

A personal note: I did this activity with my family during dinner one night. I was practicing the lesson for my money class the next day. My family has to put up with a lot. I chose the numbers 1, 2, 3, 4, 5, and 6. When we shared out, my oldest son, who was 15 at the time, became very annoyed. "No-one ever chooses those numbers!" he said.

"I did," I countered.

"Yes, but no-one else does. It's silly to choose the numbers one through six."

"Really?" I asked. "Don't I have the exact same chance of winning as you do with your six numbers?"

He knew I was right. But seeing it presented this way really underscored the message: your chance of winning is very, very, very, slim.

Bad Habits

Bad habits are expensive. Smoking, drugs, chewing tobacco… It's not just the short-term expense but the long-term health related expenses, as well. Just think how that money could grow if it was used differently. Besides, it's just not smart.

Being Poor is Expensive

It's true. Poor people spend money on things that the rest of us never need to spend money on. Think payday loans, credit card interest, check cashing fees, overdraft fees, car title loans, lottery tickets…

In addition, poor people often don't have access to health care benefits, 401(k) or other retirement plans, flexible spending plans…

So let's teach our kids to be wise with their money. It is very expensive, indeed, to be poor.

My Money Reflections – Things Your Child Should Know

Think about the activities in this chapter and answer the following questions:

☐ Have I explained to my child that using credit cards is the same as taking out a loan?

☐ Does my child understand the importance of paying credit card balances in full each month?

☐ Does my child understand that along with credit cards come responsibility and discipline?

☐ Have I played the *Chew on This* lottery activity with my family?

☐ Does my child have a basic understanding of the lottery and casino gambling and how the majority of people lose money playing them?

☐ Does my child know that there is a greater chance that he will get hit by lightning than winning the lottery?

☐ Does my child understand that not only are smoking, doing drugs, or chewing tobacco unwise choices, but it's a waste of good money that could be earning interest?

☐ Have I explained that poor people usually end up paying for fees that can add up pretty quickly and therefore have a harder time saving and making their money grow?

Chapter 10:

. . .

Money Game Plan

"Obstacles are those frightful things
you see when you take your eyes
off your goals." Henry Ford

Did you know that there's more to being good with money than paying bills on time and paying off credit cards each month? As important as these skills are, if you don't have a money game plan, you may miss out on ways to be even smarter with your money. So it's important to get kids to begin to think about how to maximize the value of their money.

In Chapter 1, we talked about your children's futures. They completed a little exercise called *My Look Into the Future* where they got to reflect on life many years out. This is a great activity to do with kids because it naturally begs the question, "And how do you plan on getting there?" And that brings us to… their money game plan.

A money game plan helps your kids decide in advance how to best handle their money…now and in the future. When we have a plan, we often perform better. We want our kids to be in control of their money, not the other way around.

If they've completed most of the activities and discussions in this book, they're ready to put their plan down on paper. Of course, just like their *My Look Into the Future*, their plans will change over time. Not a problem. We all have to revisit our plans, make adjustments and rebalance our accounts. What great training for their future.

Chew on This: My Money Game Plan

Using the worksheet *My Money Game Plan*, go over each of the questions with your child so the meaning is understood. Older kids can then write their own answers. Have younger kids dictate their answers to you.

Once the money game plan is in place, you've come full circle. I love it when that happens. And if you have any questions or comments along the way, let me know. I'd be happy to respond! karyn@kidnexions.com

May your kids go forth and multiply…their dollars!

My Money Game Plan - Sample

Most people don't plan to fail, they fail to plan.

Once you have money you need to choose what to do with it ~ you need a Money Game Plan. A Money Game Plan helps you decide in advance how to best spend the money you have now and in the future.

These are some ways I plan to earn extra money:

I plan on doing at least two extra jobs from the above-and-beyond job list. I would also like to tutor in math because I am good at it. I will make fliers and see if I can pass them out to the first and second graders at the elementary school.

This is how I will allocate (divvy-up) my money when I receive it:

I will put aside $1.00 every week for my charity. The rest will go into my savings account until I need it.

This is where I will keep my short-term savings: (piggy bank, wallet, savings account, underwear drawer)

I will keep some cash in my wallet. Then I will put the rest in my savings account at the credit union.

This is how much money I want to have before I begin investing it:

I would like to save $200 and then begin investing it.

These are some places I think I may want to invest my money: (savings account, CDs, bonds, etc.)

When I save $200 I will buy a CD. I also plan on opening a mutual fund and putting extra money into that.

This is the kind of consumer I will be: (I will look for sales, comparison shop, etc.)

I will make lists of the things I want and need and make sure that I get things that are on my list only. I will wait for sales and try and find the best store with the best prices.

If I find myself with extra money, this is what I will do with it:

If it is just a little bit, like under $10, I will put it in my wallet. Otherwise, I will deposit it into my savings account or maybe put it in my mutual fund.

This is how I plan to use credit cards when I am older:

I will always pay off my credit cards each month! I will own only two credit cards.

Signature: _____ Date: _____

My Money Game Plan

"Most people don't plan to fail, they fail to plan."

Once you have money you need to choose what to do with it ~ you need a Money Game Plan. A Money Game Plan helps you decide in advance how to best spend the money you have now and in the future.

These are some ways I plan to earn extra money:

This is how I will allocate (divvy-up) my money when I receive it:

This is where I will keep my short-term savings: (piggy bank, wallet, savings account, underwear drawer)

This is how much money I want to have before I begin investing it:

These are some places I think I may want to invest my money: (savings account, CDs, bonds, etc.)

This is the kind of consumer I will be: (I will look for sales, comparison shop, etc.)

If I find myself with extra money, this is what I will do with it:

This is how I plan to use credit cards when I am older:

Signature: _____ Date: _____

My Money Reflections – Money Game Plan

Think about the activities in this chapter and answer the following questions:

☐ Does my child understand that the choices she makes now with her money will affect her future?

☐ Have I discussed with my child what he plans on doing with his money when he receives it?

☐ Have I helped my child reflect on the type of consumer she will be? (making purchases, credit card use, gambling)

☐ Does my child understand that when he receives money he has choices about what to do with it?

☐ Has my child completed the *My Money Game Plan?*

Glossary

active income: money earned for services

balance: the amount of money left in your account

bank: an institution that holds money for individuals and businesses

bonds: loans to the local, state, or federal government, or even a corporation

borrow: using someone else's money with the intent of paying it back

budget: a plan for your money, how much you bring in and how it will be spent and saved

certificate of deposit: time-based, fixed rate of return investment

check: a written form of payment which draws the money from the issuer's checking account

checking account: an account from a bank or credit union that allows you to write checks

compound interest: interest earned on the original amount plus the interest already accumulated

consumer: a person who buys goods or services

credit card: a card that allows people to purchase items with the intent of paying it off. The balance on a credit card will accrue interest if not paid off in full each month.

credit report: a report about an individual's credit history that is used to determine a person's financial reliability

credit union: a financial cooperative which is owned by its members which holds money for individuals

debit card: a card that allows money to be immediately drawn from an individual's account

deposit: the act of adding money to an individual's account

diversify: to invest in a variety of investments such as stocks, mutual funds, real estate, in order to reduce overall risk

dividends: the profits given by a company to its stockholders

earn: to acquire by labor, service, or performance

entrepreneur: someone who creates a business and assumes the risk for it

expense: an amount paid for goods or services

finance charge: the cost of credit or borrowing money

gambling: taking a risk in the hopes of gaining

goods: material products that are purchased

growth rate: percentage rate at which investments are growing

income: money earned by working or from investments

interest: 1) a fee paid on borrowed money; 2) the money earned on investments

invest: to put money into an enterprise with the hopes of making a profit

investment: an enterprise, such as stocks or real estate, that is used with the intent of making a profit

loan: borrowing with the intent of giving back; borrowing money which needs to be repaid with interest

long-term goal: a goal that usually goes out several or more years

lottery: a game of chance where people purchase tickets and hope to win a lot of money usually by some kind of drawing

media literacy: the ability to critique and analyze messages being sent to us through the media

money market fund: a mutual fund that buys short-term, low risk securities

mutual funds: a collection of stocks and bonds made up from a pool of funds

need: something you depend on

negotiate: to discuss options with someone else in order to reach agreement

opportunity cost: giving up the next best option as the result of getting something else

passive income: income that does not require your direct involvement

profit: total income minus expenses

raise: an increase in salary or wages

registry: a written record of income, expenses, and balance

save: to put money aside for future use

savings account: an account with a bank or credit union which pays interest or dividends on balances held

securities: stocks, bonds, and other tradable financial assets

services: tasks done by people that others pay for

short-term goal: a goal whose timeline is usually less than a year or two

stock certificate: a certificate representing one unit of ownership in a company

tween: a child between the ages of 8 - 12

want: something we desire but do not need

6176466R0

Made in the USA
Charleston, SC
23 September 2010